FARMHOUSE
COOKING

FARMHOUSE COOKING

the best of country home cooking with
200 fresh and seasonal recipes shown
step-by-step in over 700 photographs

EDITOR LIZ TRIGG

JG
PRESS

Published by World Publications Group, Inc.
140 Laurel Street, East Bridgewater, MA 02333
www.wrldpub.net

Produced by Anness Publishing Ltd
Hermes House, 88–89 Blackfriars Road, London SE1 8HA
tel. 020 7401 2077; fax 020 7633 9499
www.annesspublishing.com

If you like the images in this book and would like to investigate using them for publishing, promotions or advertising, please visit our website www.practicalpictures.com for more information.

Publisher: Joanna Lorenz
Project Editor: Gaby Goldsack
Editor: Jenni Fleetwood
Designer: Siân Keogh, Axis Design
Illustrator: Anna Koska

ETHICAL TRADING POLICY

Because of our ongoing ecological investment program, you, as our customer, can have the pleasure and reassurance of knowing that a tree is being cultivated on your behalf to naturally replace the materials used to make the book you are holding. For further information about this scheme, go to www.annesspublishing.com/trees

The publishers would like to thank the following contributors:
Carla Capalbo, Jacqueline Clark, Maxine Clark Cleary, Carole Clements, Stephanie Donaldson,
Joanna Farrow, Christine France, Christine Ingram,
Judy Jackson, Patricia Lousada, Norma MacMillan, Katherine Richmond,
Laura Washburn, Steven Wheeler, Elizabeth Wolf-Cohen.
They would also like to thank the following photographers:
Karl Adamson, Edward Allwright, James Duncan, John Freeman, Michelle Garrett,
Amanda Heywood, Patrick McLeavey.

ISBN-10: 1-57215-513-2
ISBN-13: 978-1-57215-513-8

Printed and bound in China

Previously published as *The Farmhouse Cookbook*

Contents

Introduction

The essence of farmhouse cooking is not dependent on geography; it can be enjoyed whether you live in a country cottage or an urban townhouse. This book is full of mouthwatering recipes that can be enjoyed in any locality. Throughout, the emphasis is on fresh country foods that provide wholesome country fare. Whether you are out to impress special guests or simply want to create a wholesome meal to fill your family after a long, hard day, the recipes in this book will give you plenty of rustic meals to choose from.

Farmhouse Cooking

Some of the finest cooking in the world is to be found in farmhouses. Whether they are sited alongside orchards, among vineyards, on the prairie or along green hills, one factor will be constant—the kitchen will be the heart of the homestead.

A love of good food is common to all country folk. Working the land is one of the finest ways of stimulating the appetite, and what better way to satisfy hunger than to enjoy a fine meal, flavored with freshly picked herbs and served with fresh vegetables straight from the kitchen garden?

It is this availability of first-class raw materials that has given farmhouse cooking its essential character: by and large it is simple, satisfying food with few frills. When you can wander between rows of salad makings, lifting a lettuce here, a bunch of radishes there, then pause to pick a few young sorrel leaves and some chives, your salad will not need an elaborate dressing. When pick-your-own means literally that, and you can combine your very own strawberries with cream from cows you know by name, you have the means of making a dessert no restaurant could better.

Of course, there are some drawbacks. Unlike the town dweller, who can pop into a supermarket for produce from all around the world all through the year, the farmhouse cook tends to use whatever he or she has on hand. Perhaps that is no bad thing. Many of us have forgotten the pleasure of shelling the first peas or digging up early potatoes so tiny and tasty that it seems sacrilege even to add butter to them. When asparagus is not something you can have whenever you want, but is a rare treat in a short season, it becomes all the more special.

Farmhouse cooks step beyond their own gardens and get to know the riches of the countryside, too. They gather mushrooms and hazelnuts, know where there are blueberry bushes to be found, and pick wild blackberries for making pies and cobblers.

The farming year is punctuated with festivals. Easter is marked with special breads and cakes; a popular centerpiece for thanksgiving is a loaf of freshly baked bread; and the coming of Christmas is an excuse for a positive orgy of baking, as cookies, puddings and cakes are prepared, along with pickles and chutneys for days of feasting.

Farmhouse cooks like nothing more than a celebration, and are never happier than when cooking for a crowd. Depending on the country—and the season—dining rooms will be dusted or tables taken into the garden, flowers will be picked, wine mulled or chilled, and enough food cooked to feed a small army. And if extra guests arrive unexpectedly, so much the better—after all, there'll be plenty of food to go around.

Farmhouse food is celebrated in this book. You'll find pâtés, pies and pickles within its pages, alongside substantial stews and simple salads. Some of the dishes are slow-cooked for melting tenderness, others are swift solutions to those occasions when there's little time for complicated cooking—and all are utterly delicious!

LEFT: *The harvest loaf is a potent symbol of country life.*
OPPOSITE: *The farmhouse cook relies on fresh seasonal produce.*

The Farmhouse Kitchen Garden

If the kitchen is the heart of the farmhouse, the kitchen garden is what supplies its strength. Having fresh herbs and vegetables within easy reach makes all the difference to country cooking. A bouquet garni that consists of fresh parsley, thyme and bay gives so much more flavor than something that resembles a tea bag, and gathering the herbs from your own plants is supremely satisfying.

Of course, you don't have to live in a farmhouse to reap the benefits of your own kitchen garden. A small sunny plot near the kitchen door is ideal, but you can garden in tubs or even pots on the windowsill.

Growing your own herbs gives you a wonderful opportunity to experiment with some of the more unusual varieties. Specialty herb growers have a wide range of young plants in pots, and are usually so enthusiastic about their produce that they will not only give growing tips, but will also share favorite recipes. Seed catalogs are a good source of supply, too, and a good way of involving younger members of the family. Children enjoy choosing and planting their own seeds, and are far less likely to be fussy about trying dishes flavored with herbs when they have grown them themselves. The same goes for vegetables—involve children in the cultivation and the cooking (and eating) will come naturally.

PLANTING SEEDS
Every packet of seeds carries instructions for planting. If you are growing herbs and salad greens for the windowsill, you can germinate seeds in partitioned trays and transfer the plants, as they grow, to well-drained pots until they are large enough to be planted in the garden. Regular watering and plenty of sun will ensure an abundance of freshness and flavor.

Tomatoes can be grown from seed, but many gardeners prefer to buy young plants. Tomato plants do well in growing bags on a patio and are best positioned against a south-facing wall. Vegetables such as carrots, radishes, beets and turnips are best planted in rich soil in an open bed. Seedlings that grow too close together should be thinned to allow for proper development. Young vegetables are delicious in fresh, colorful salads.

GROWING IN POTS
Salad greens and herbs can be grown successfully in terra-cotta pots. Regular watering is important, but you should check the seed package or a gardening book to determine how much. Some herbs love water, but many Mediterranean plants prefer it if the soil is left until it is almost dry before being given a thorough soaking. All pots should allow for drainage.

For a constant supply of lettuce, sow seeds at two-week intervals throughout the summer and pick when needed (many new varieties allow you to take only as many leaves as you require, while the plant continues to grow). In colder weather, herbs and salad greens should be kept under glass to maximize warmth from the sun. Many herbs enjoy a sunny spot on an inside window ledge.

PICKING AND STORING HERBS
Ideally, herbs should be used as soon as they are picked. If this is not possible, store them with care. In season, bunches of parsley, mint, cilantro and chives keep well in pitchers of water in the refrigerator. Cover the top of each pitcher with a plastic bag. Thyme, rosemary, lavender and bay leaves can be tied in bunches and hung in a well-ventilated pantry to dry. Dried herbs will keep for several months.

French Dressing with Herbs

An herb dressing makes the perfect partner for a simple green salad.

INGREDIENTS

*¼ cup extra virgin olive oil
2 tablespoons peanut or sunflower oil
1 tablespoon lemon juice
¼ cup finely chopped fresh herbs, such as parsley, chives, tarragon and marjoram
pinch of sugar*

Makes about ½ cup

1

Place the olive and peanut or sunflower oil in a screw-top jar.

2

Add the lemon juice, herbs and sugar. Screw on the lid and shake well.

TOP LEFT: *Grow seeds in small trays on the windowsill, then transplant to individual pots. When large enough, plant them in the garden.*

ABOVE AND TOP RIGHT: *Store chives and Italian parsley in a water-filled jar in the refrigerator. Lavender and thyme can be tied in bunches and dried.*

Making Meat Stock

As every farmhouse cook will tell you, good homemade stock is the secret of successful meat soups, stews, casseroles, gravies and sauces.

INGREDIENTS

4–4½ pounds beef bones, such as shin, leg, neck and shoulder, or veal or lamb bones, cut into 2½-inch pieces
2 onions, unpeeled, quartered
2 carrots, roughly chopped
2 celery stalks, with leaves if possible, roughly chopped
2 tomatoes, coarsely chopped

4 quarts water
a handful of parsley stalks
a few fresh thyme sprigs or ¾ teaspoon dried thyme
2 bay leaves
10 black peppercorns, lightly crushed

Makes about 4 quarts

1

Preheat the oven to 450°F. Put the bones in a roasting pan or flameproof casserole and roast, turning occasionally, for 30 minutes or until they start to brown.

2

Add the vegetables and baste with the fat in the pan or casserole. Roast for another 20–30 minutes or until the bones are well browned. Stir and baste occasionally.

3

Transfer the bones and vegetables to a stockpot. Spoon off the fat from the roasting pan or casserole, add a little water and bring to a boil, scraping in any residue. Pour this liquid into the stockpot.

4

Add the remaining water. Bring just to a boil, skimming frequently to remove any foam. Add the herbs and peppercorns.

5

Partly cover the pot and simmer the stock for 4–6 hours, adding the liquid as necessary.

6

Strain the stock. Skim as much fat as possible from the surface. If possible, cool the stock and then chill it; the fat will set in a layer on the surface and can be removed easily.

Making Chicken Stock

Use turkey to make the stock, if you prefer.

INGREDIENTS

*2½–3 pounds chicken wings, backs
and necks
2 onions, unpeeled, quartered
4 quarts water
2 carrots, roughly chopped
2 celery stalks, with leaves if possible,
roughly chopped
a small handful of fresh parsley
a few fresh thyme sprigs or ¾ teaspoon
dried thyme
1 or 2 bay leaves
10 black peppercorns, lightly crushed*

Makes about 2½ quarts

1

Put the chicken pieces and the onions in a
stockpot. Cook over medium heat, stirring
occasionally, until lightly browned. Stir in
the water. Bring to a boil. Skim the surface.

2

Add the remaining ingredients. Simmer for
3 hours. Strain, cool and chill. When cold,
remove the fat from the surface.

Making Vegetable Stock

Vary the ingredients for this fresh-flavored stock according to what you have on hand.

INGREDIENTS

*2 large onions, coarsely chopped
2 leeks, sliced
3 garlic cloves, crushed
3 carrots, coarsely chopped
4 celery stalks, coarsely chopped
1 large strip of pared lemon rind
a handful of parsley stalks
a few fresh thyme sprigs
2 bay leaves
3½ quarts water*

Makes 3½ quarts

1

Put the vegetables, lemon rind, herbs and
water in a stockpot and bring to a boil.
Skim the surface.

2

Reduce the heat and simmer, uncovered, for
30 minutes. Strain the stock and let cool.

Soups
and Appetizers

In the farmhouse kitchen, stock simmers on the stove, ready to form the basis of a nourishing soup to satisfy appetites honed by hard work and an early start. When the harvest is in, there'll be time for more leisurely meals, prefaced by cheeses, pâtés and simple salads. The following selection of delicious soups and appetizers has been selected from farmhouse kitchens around the world. There are recipes to suit all occasions and tastes, from simple country soups to sophisticated pâtés.

Country Vegetable Soup

This satisfying soup captures all the flavors of the countryside. The basil and garlic purée gives it extra color and a wonderful aroma—so don't omit it.

INGREDIENTS

1½ cups fresh shelled fava beans, or
¾ cup dried great northern beans,
soaked overnight in water to cover
½ teaspoon dried herbes de Provence
2 garlic cloves, finely chopped
1 tablespoon olive oil
1 onion, finely chopped
2 small leeks, finely sliced
1 celery stalk, finely sliced
2 carrots, finely diced
2 small potatoes, peeled and finely diced
4 ounces green beans
5 cups water
1 cup peas, fresh or frozen
2 small zucchini, finely chopped
3 tomatoes, skinned, seeded and finely chopped
a handful of spinach leaves, cut into thin ribbons
salt and freshly ground black pepper
fresh basil sprigs, to garnish

For the garlic purée
1 or 2 garlic cloves, finely chopped
½ cup basil leaves
¼ cup grated Parmesan cheese
¼ cup extra virgin olive oil

Serves 6–8

NOTE
To serve the soup, season and swirl a spoonful of purée into each bowl and garnish with basil.

1

To make the purée, process the garlic, basil and Parmesan until smooth. With the machine running, slowly add the olive oil through the feed-tube. Alternatively, put the garlic, basil and cheese in a mortar. Pound with a pestle, then stir in the oil.

3

Heat the oil in a saucepan. Fry the onion and leeks for 5 minutes, stirring occasionally.

5

Add the potatoes, green beans and water. Bring to a boil, then cover and simmer for 10 minutes.

2

If using dried beans, boil vigorously for 10 minutes and drain. Place them or the fresh beans in a saucepan with the herbs and 1 chopped garlic clove. Add water to cover by 1 inch. Bring to a boil and simmer for 10 minutes for fresh beans or about 1 hour for dried beans. Set aside.

4

Add the celery and carrots, with the remaining garlic clove. Cook for 10 minutes.

6

Add the peas, zucchini and tomatoes, with the reserved beans. Simmer for 25–30 minutes. Add the spinach, season to taste, and simmer for 5 minutes.

Herb and Chili Gazpacho

Gazpacho is a lovely soup, set off perfectly by the addition of a few herbs.

INGREDIENTS

2½ pounds ripe tomatoes
8 ounces onions
2 green peppers
1 green chili
1 large cucumber
2 tablespoons red wine vinegar
1 tablespoon balsamic vinegar
2 tablespoons olive oil
1 clove of garlic, peeled and crushed
⅓ cup tomato juice
2 tablespoons tomato paste
salt and pepper
2 tablespoons finely chopped mixed
fresh herbs, plus some extra to garnish

Serves 6

1

Set aside about a quarter of all the fresh vegetables, except the green chili, and place all the remaining ingredients in a food processor and season to taste. Process finely and chill in the refrigerator.

2

Chop the remaining vegetables and serve in a separate bowl to sprinkle over the soup. Crush some ice cubes and add to the center of each bowl. Garnish with fresh herbs. Serve with bread rolls.

Pear and Watercress Soup with Stilton Croutons

Pears and Stilton taste very good when you eat them together after the main course—here, for a change, they are served as an appetizer.

INGREDIENTS

1 bunch watercress
4 medium pears, sliced
6 cups chicken stock, preferably homemade
salt and pepper
½ cup heavy cream
juice of 1 lime

For the croutons
2 tablespoons butter
1 tablespoon olive oil
2 cups cubed stale bread
5 ounces chopped Stilton cheese

Serves 6

1

Set aside about a third of the watercress leaves. Place all the rest of the watercress leaves and stalks in a pan with the pears, stock and a little seasoning. Simmer for 15–20 minutes.

2

Reserving some watercress leaves for garnishing, add the rest of the leaves and immediately blend in a food processor until smooth.

3

Put the mixture in a bowl and stir in the cream and lime juice to mix the flavors thoroughly. Season again to taste. Pour all the soup back into a pan and reheat, stirring gently until warmed through.

4

To make the croutons, melt the butter and oil and fry the bread cubes until golden brown. Drain on paper towels. Put the cheese on top and heat under a hot broiler until bubbling. Reheat the soup and pour into bowls. Divide the croutons and remaining watercress among the bowls.

Green Bean Soup with Parmesan

Make the most of a garden glut of green beans by serving this colorful summer soup.

INGREDIENTS

2 teaspoons butter
8 ounces green beans, trimmed
1 garlic clove, crushed
2 cups vegetable stock
⅔ cup Parmesan cheese
¼ cup light cream or
half-and-half
2 tablespoons chopped fresh parsley
salt and freshly ground black pepper

Serves 4

1

Melt the butter in a saucepan and cook the green beans and garlic for 2–3 minutes over medium heat, stirring frequently. Stir in the stock with salt and pepper to taste. Bring to a boil. Reduce the heat and simmer for 10–15 minutes, until the beans are tender.

2

Process the soup until smooth. Alternatively, purée the soup in a food mill. Return it to the clean pan and heat gently. Stir in the Parmesan and cream. Sprinkle with the parsley and serve.

Lentil and Vegetable Soup

Unlike red lentils, the brown variety retains its shape after cooking and add texture to this hearty country soup.

INGREDIENTS

1 cup brown lentils
4 cups chicken stock
1 cup water
¼ cup dry red wine
1½ pounds tomatoes, skinned, seeded
and chopped, or 1 can (14 ounces)
chopped tomatoes
1 carrot, sliced
1 onion, chopped
1 celery stalk, sliced
1 garlic clove, crushed
¼ teaspoon ground coriander
2 teaspoons snipped fresh basil, or
½ teaspoon dried basil
1 bay leaf
6 tablespoons freshly grated Parmesan
cheese

Serves 6

1

Put the lentils in a sieve. Rinse under cold running water, then discard any discolored ones and any grit.

3

Reduce the heat to low, cover and simmer for 20–25 minutes, stirring occasionally. When the lentils are tender, discard the bay leaf and ladle the soup into 6 warmed bowls. Sprinkle each portion with 1 tablespoon of the Parmesan.

2

Put the lentils in a large saucepan. Add all the remaining ingredients, except the Parmesan, and bring to a boil.

NOTE

For a more substantial soup, add about ½ cup finely chopped cooked ham for the last 10 minutes of cooking.

Borscht

This rustic soup was the staple diet of prerevolutionary Russian peasants for centuries.
There are many variations—it is rare to find two identical recipes.

INGREDIENTS

6 whole, uncooked beets
1 tablespoon sunflower oil
4 ounces lean bacon strips, chopped
1 large onion
1 large carrot, cut into short thin
sticks
3 celery stalks, thinly sliced
6 cups chicken stock
6–8 ounces tomatoes, skinned, seeded
and sliced
about 2 tablespoons lemon juice or wine
vinegar
2 tablespoons chopped fresh dill
½ medium white cabbage, thinly sliced
⅔ cup sour cream
salt and freshly ground black pepper

Serves 6

1

Peel the beets, slice and then cut into very
thin strips. Heat the oil in a large, heavy
saucepan and fry the bacon over gentle heat
for 3–4 minutes.

2

Add the onion to the pan, fry for
2–3 minutes and then add the carrot, celery
and beet. Cook for 4–5 minutes, stirring
frequently, until the oil has been absorbed.

3

Add the stock, tomatoes, lemon juice or
wine vinegar and half of the dill. Season,
then bring to a boil, lower the heat and
simmer for about 30–40 minutes, until the
vegetables are completely tender.

4

Add the cabbage and simmer for 5 minutes,
or until tender. Adjust the seasoning and
serve, swirled with the sour cream and
sprinkled with the remaining dill.

Farmhouse Onion Soup

Slow, careful cooking is the secret of this traditional onion soup.

INGREDIENTS

*2 tablespoons sunflower or olive oil, or
a mixture
2 tablespoons butter
4 large onions, chopped
4 cups beef stock
4 slices French bread
1¹/₂–2 ounces Gruyère or Cheddar
cheese, grated
salt and freshly ground black pepper*

Serves 4

1

Heat the oil and butter in a deep saucepan and fry the onions briskly for 3–4 minutes. Reduce the heat and cook gently for 45–60 minutes.

2

When the onions are a rich mahogany brown, add the beef stock and a little seasoning. Simmer, partially covered, for 30 minutes, then taste and adjust the seasoning.

3

Preheat the broiler and toast the French bread. Spoon the soup into four soup dishes that can safely be used under the broiler. Place a piece of bread in each. Sprinkle with the cheese and broil for a few minutes, until golden.

Summer Tomato Soup

The success of this soup depends on using ripe, full-flavored tomatoes, such as the oval plum variety. It is traditionally made when the tomato season is at its peak.

INGREDIENTS

*1 tablespoon olive oil
1 large onion, chopped
1 carrot, chopped
2¼ pounds ripe tomatoes, cored and quartered
2 garlic cloves, chopped
5 fresh thyme sprigs
4 or 5 fresh marjoram sprigs, plus extra for garnish
1 bay leaf
3 tablespoons sour cream or yogurt, plus a little extra to garnish
salt and freshly ground black pepper*

Serves 4

1

Heat the olive oil in a large saucepan. Cook the onion and carrot over medium heat for 3–4 minutes, until just softened, stirring occasionally.

2

Add the tomatoes, garlic and herbs. Simmer, covered, for 30 minutes, then sieve the soup into a clean pan. Stir in the sour cream or yogurt and season. Reheat gently and serve garnished with cream or yogurt and marjoram.

Pumpkin Soup

When the first frosts of autumn chill the air, bright orange pumpkins are a vivid sight in gardens and at country markets. Pumpkin soup is delicious.

INGREDIENTS

*2 tablespoons butter
1 large onion, chopped
2 shallots, chopped
2 potatoes, peeled and cubed
6 cups cubed pumpkin flesh
8 cups chicken or vegetable stock
½ teaspoon ground cumin
pinch of freshly grated nutmeg
salt and freshly ground black pepper
fresh parsley or chives, to garnish*

Serves 6–8

1

Melt the butter in a large saucepan and cook the onion and shallots for 4–5 minutes, until just softened. Add the potatoes, pumpkin, stock and spices with a little salt and black pepper. Simmer, covered, for about 1 hour, stirring occasionally.

2

With a slotted spoon, transfer the cooked vegetables to a food processor. Process until smooth, adding a little of the cooking liquid if needed. Stir the purée into the cooking liquid remaining in the pan. Adjust the seasoning and reheat gently. Serve garnished with the fresh herbs.

Barley Soup

A feature of the farmhouse kitchen is the stockpot simmering on the stove. With a good homemade stock on hand, it only takes a few simple ingredients to make an excellent soup.

INGREDIENTS

2 pounds meaty soup bones (lamb, beef or veal)
4 cups water
2 tablespoons oil
3 carrots, finely chopped
4 celery stalks, finely sliced
1 onion, finely chopped
2 tablespoons pearl barley
salt and freshly ground black pepper

Serves 4

NOTE

All soups taste better with homemade stock. The long, slow simmering can be done well in advance and stocks freeze well. A quick version of this soup can be made using water and a bouillon cube, but it won't have the same flavor.

1

Preheat the oven to 400°F. To prepare the meat stock, brown the lamb, beef or veal bones in a roasting pan in the oven for about 30 minutes. Put the bones in a large saucepan, cover with the water and bring to a boil.

2

Use a metal spoon to skim off the surface froth, then cover the pan and simmer the stock for at least 2 hours. Heat the oil in a saucepan and sauté the carrots, celery and onion for about 1 minute. Strain the stock into the pan.

3

Add the barley to the pan of vegetables and continue cooking for about 1 hour, until the barley is soft. Season the soup with plenty of salt and pepper, transfer to serving bowls and serve hot.

Bacon and Lentil Soup

Serve this hearty soup with chunks of warm, crusty bread.

INGREDIENTS

*1 lb thick-sliced bacon,
cubed
1 onion, coarsely chopped
1 small turnip, coarsely chopped
1 celery stalk, chopped
1 carrot, sliced
1 potato, peeled and
coarsely chopped
½ cup lentils
1 bouquet garni
freshly ground black pepper*

Serves 4

1

Heat a large pan and add the bacon. Cook for
a few minutes, allowing the fat to run out.

2

Add all the vegetables and cook for
4 minutes.

3

Add the lentils, bouquet garni, seasoning
and enough water to cover. Bring to a boil
and simmer for 1 hour, or until the lentils
are tender.

Stuffed Grape Leaves with Garlic Yogurt

This is the perfect appetizer to set the scene for one of those long summer lunches in the garden.

INGREDIENTS

1 jar (8 ounces) preserved grape leaves
1 onion, finely chopped
½ bunch scallions, finely chopped
¼ cup chopped fresh parsley
10 large fresh mint sprigs, chopped
finely grated zest of 1 lemon
½ teaspoon crushed dried chilies
1½ teaspoons fennel seeds, crushed
1 cup long-grain rice
½ cup olive oil
1¼ cups boiling water
⅔ cup thick plain yogurt
2 garlic cloves, crushed
salt
lemon wedges and mint leaves, to
garnish (optional)

Serves 6

1

Rinse the grape leaves well, then soak
them in boiling water for 10 minutes.
Meanwhile, mix the onion, scallions, herbs,
lemon zest, chilies, fennel seeds and rice
with 1½ tablespoons of the olive oil. Season
with salt.

2

Drain the grape leaves. Place a leaf, veins
uppermost, on a work surface and cut off
any stalk. Place a heaping teaspoonful of
the rice mixture near the stalk end. Fold
the stalk end over the filling, then fold over
the sides. Roll into a cigar shape. Repeat
with the remaining leaves and filling.

3

Place any remaining leaves in the bottom of
a heavy saucepan. Pack the stuffed leaves in
a single layer in the pan. Spoon the
remaining oil over them, then add the
measured boiling water.

4

Place a small plate over the leaves to keep
them submerged. Cover and cook over
very low heat for 45 minutes. Meanwhile,
mix the yogurt and garlic in a small
serving dish. Transfer the stuffed leaves to a
serving plate and garnish with lemon
wedges and mint, if desired. Serve with the
garlic yogurt.

Stuffed Garlic Mushrooms

Flavorful portobello mushrooms make a simply delicious appetizer when stuffed and baked.

INGREDIENTS

1 onion, chopped
6 tablespoons butter
8 portobello mushrooms of similar size
¼ cup wild or dried mushrooms, soaked
in warm water for 20 minutes
1 garlic clove, crushed
1½ cups fresh bread crumbs
1 egg
5 tablespoons chopped fresh parsley
1 tablespoon chopped fresh thyme
4 ounces prosciutto, thinly sliced
salt and freshly ground black pepper
fresh parsley, to garnish

Serves 4

1

Preheat the oven to 375°F. Fry the onions gently in half the butter until soft. Break off the stems of the portobello mushrooms, setting the caps aside. Drain the dried or wild mushrooms and chop these and the portobello mushroom stems finely. Add to the onion, with the garlic, and cook for 2–3 minutes more.

2

Put the mixture in a bowl and add the bread crumbs, egg, herbs and seasoning. Melt the remaining butter and brush it over the mushroom caps. Arrange them on a baking sheet and spoon in the filling. Bake for 20–30 minutes, until well browned. Top each mushroom with a strip of prosciutto, garnish with parsley and serve.

Mushroom Salad with Prosciutto

Ribbons of ham and pancake, tossed with wild mushrooms and salad greens,
provide a feast for the eyes and the palate.

INGREDIENTS

3 tablespoons butter
1 pound assorted wild and cultivated
mushrooms, sliced
¼ cup sherry
juice of ½ lemon
mixed lettuce greens
2 tablespoons walnut oil
6 ounces prosciutto, cut into ribbons

For the pancake ribbons
¼ cup all-purpose flour
5 tablespoons milk
1 egg
¼ cup grated Parmesan cheese
¼ cup chopped fresh herbs
salt and freshly ground black pepper

Serves 4

1

To make the pancakes, mix the flour and milk in a bowl. Beat in the egg, cheese, herbs and seasoning. Pour enough of the mixture into a hot, greased frying pan to coat the bottom of it. When set, turn the pancake over and cook briefly on the other side. Cool, then roll up and slice into ribbons. Repeat with the remaining batter.

2

Cook the mushrooms in the butter for 6–8 minutes. Add the sherry and lemon juice, and season to taste.

3

Toss the lettuce in the oil and arrange on plates. Place the prosciutto and pancake ribbons in the center and spoon on the mushrooms.

Mushroom Picker's Pâté

One of the delights of country living is to rise early and go on a mushrooming expedition with an expert who knows precisely what mushrooms are edible. This pâté is the perfect reward.

INGREDIENTS

3 tablespoons vegetable oil
1 onion, chopped
½ celery stalk, chopped
12 ounces mushrooms, sliced
⅔ cup red lentils
2 cups water or vegetable stock
1 fresh thyme sprig

¼ cup almond or
cashew butter
1 garlic clove, crushed
1 thick slice white bread, crusts removed
5 tablespoons milk
1 tablespoon lemon juice
4 egg yolks
celery salt and ground black pepper

Serves 6

1

Preheat the oven to 350°F. Brown the onion and celery in the oil. Add the mushrooms and soften for 3–4 minutes. Remove a spoonful of the mushroom pieces and set it aside.

2

Add the lentils, water or stock and thyme to the mushroom mixture. Bring to a boil, then lower the heat and simmer for 20 minutes, or until the lentils are very soft.

3

Place the nut butter, garlic, bread and milk in a food processor and process until smooth.

4

Add the lemon juice and egg yolks and process briefly. Add the lentil mixture, process until smooth, then season with the celery salt and pepper. Lastly, stir the reserved mushrooms into the mixture.

5

Spoon the mixture into a 5-cup pâté dish and cover with foil. Set the dish in a roasting pan and pour in boiling water to come halfway up the sides of the dish. Cook the pâté for 50 minutes. Allow to cool before serving.

NOTE
If you are using only cultivated mushrooms, the addition of 3 tablespoons of dried porcini will boost the flavor. Soak the dried mushrooms in warm water for 20 minutes before draining and adding to the pan with the fresh mushrooms.

Country-style Pâté with Leeks

A rough pâté is very much a feature of the farmhouse kitchen. Cooked slowly so that all the flavors combine, then pressed, it makes a perfect appetizer or light lunch.

INGREDIENTS

1 tablespoon butter
1 pound leeks (white and pale green parts), sliced
2 or 3 large garlic cloves, finely chopped
2¼ pounds lean pork leg or shoulder, trimmed and cubed
5 ounces lean bacon strips
1½ teaspoons chopped fresh thyme
3 fresh sage leaves, finely chopped
¼ teaspoon quatre épices (mixed ground cloves, cinnamon, nutmeg and black pepper)
¼ teaspoon ground cumin
pinch of freshly grated nutmeg
½ teaspoon salt
1 teaspoon freshly ground black pepper
1 bay leaf

Serves 8–10

1

Melt the butter in a large, heavy saucepan, add the leeks, then cover and sweat over a low heat for 10 minutes, stirring occasionally. Add the garlic and continue cooking for about 10 minutes, until the leeks are very soft, then set aside to cool.

2

Pulse the meat cubes in batches in a food processor to chop it coarsely. Alternatively, pass the meat through the coarse blade of a mincer. Transfer the meat to a large mixing bowl and remove any white stringy bits. Reserve two of the bacon strips for garnishing, then chop or grind the remainder, and mix with the pork in the mixing bowl.

3

Preheat the oven to 350°F. Line the bottom and sides of a 6-cup terrine with waxed paper or parchment paper. Add the leek mixture, herbs and spices to the pork mixture, with the salt and pepper.

4

Spoon the mixture into the terrine, pressing it into the corners and compacting it. Tap firmly to settle the mixture and smooth the top. Arrange the bay leaf and bacon strips on top, then cover tightly with foil.

5

Place the terrine in a roasting pan and pour in boiling water to come halfway up the side. Bake for 1¼ hours. Drain off the water, then return the terrine to the roasting pan and place a baking sheet on top. Weight with two or three large cans or a foil-wrapped clean brick while the pâté cools. Chill overnight, before slicing.

Roasted Bell Pepper Medley

When roasted, red bell peppers acquire a marvelous smoky flavor that is wonderful with sun-dried tomatoes and artichoke hearts.

INGREDIENTS

½ cup drained sun-dried tomatoes in
oil
3 red bell peppers
2 yellow or orange bell peppers
2 green bell peppers
2 tablespoons balsamic vinegar
a few drops of chili sauce

5 tablespoons olive oil
4 drained, canned artichoke hearts,
sliced
1 garlic clove, thinly sliced
salt and freshly ground black pepper
fresh basil leaves, to garnish

Serves 6

1

Preheat the oven to 400°F. Slice the sun-dried tomatoes into thin strips. Set aside. Put the whole peppers on an oiled baking sheet and bake for about 45 minutes, until beginning to char. Cover with a dish towel and let cool for 5 minutes.

2

Mix the vinegar and chili sauce in a bowl. Whisk in the oil, then season with a little salt and pepper.

3

Peel and slice the peppers. Mix with the artichokes, tomatoes and garlic in a bowl. Toss with the dressing and scatter with the basil leaves.

Baby Eggplants with Raisins and Pine Nuts

Make this simple appetizer a day in advance, to allow the sweet and sour flavors to develop.

INGREDIENTS

1 cup extra virgin olive oil
juice of 1 lemon
2 tablespoons balsamic vinegar
3 cloves
⅓ cup pine nuts
3 tablespoons raisins
1 tablespoon sugar
1 bay leaf
large pinch of dried chili flakes
12 baby eggplants, halved lengthwise
salt and freshly ground black pepper

Serves 4

TIP
Use sliced eggplants if baby ones are not obtainable, or try this with grilled peppers.

1

Put ¾ cup of the olive oil in a bowl. Add the lemon juice, vinegar, cloves, pine nuts, raisins, sugar and bay leaf. Stir in the chili flakes and salt and pepper. Mix well. Preheat the broiler.

2

Brush the eggplants with the remaining oil. Broil for 10 minutes, until slightly blackened, turning them over halfway through. Place the hot eggplants in a bowl, and pour the marinade on top. Let cool, turning the eggplants once or twice. Serve at room temperature.

Cheese and Potato Patties

Serve these delicious little potato cakes with a simple tomato salad for an inexpensive but imaginative appetizer.

INGREDIENTS

1¼ pounds potatoes
4 ounces feta or Roquefort cheese
4 scallions, finely chopped
3 tablespoons chopped fresh dill
1 egg, beaten
1 tablespoon lemon juice
all-purpose flour, for dredging
3 tablespoons olive oil
salt and freshly ground black pepper

Serves 4

TIP
Add salt sparingly when making the potato cakes, as the cheese will be salty.

1

Boil the potatoes in their skins in a saucepan of lightly salted water until soft. Drain, peel and mash while still warm. Crumble the feta cheese or Roquefort into the potatoes and add the scallions, dill, egg and lemon juice. Season with salt and pepper. Stir well.

2

Cover the mixture and chill until firm. Divide the mixture into walnut-sized balls, then flatten them slightly. Dredge with flour. Heat the oil in a frying pan and fry the potato patties until golden brown on each side. Drain on paper towels and serve at once.

Fonduta

Fontina is an Italian medium-fat cheese with a rich salty flavor, a little like Gruyère, which is a good substitute. This delicious hot dip makes a good appetizer before a fairly light main course. Serve it with warm crusty bread.

INGREDIENTS

9 ounces fontina or Gruyère cheese,
1 cup milk
1 tablespoon butter
2 eggs, lightly beaten
freshly ground black pepper

Serves 4

1

2

NOTE
Do not overheat the sauce, or the eggs may curdle. A very gentle heat will produce a lovely smooth sauce.

Put the cheese in a bowl with the milk and soak for 2–3 hours. Transfer to a double boiler or a heatproof bowl set over a pan of simmering water.

Add the butter and eggs and cook gently, stirring, until the cheese has melted to a smooth sauce with the consistency of custard. Remove from the heat, season with pepper and serve in a warmed serving dish.

Vegetables

Farmhouse cooks really know their vegetables. They tend to cook by the season, picking or pulling up the first young vegetables as soon as they are ready, and turning them into superb side dishes, salads and vegetarian meals. The following section is a selection of delicious recipes inspired by the rural tradition. Some of the recipes are for hearty main dishes, while others are designed as flavorful side dishes. To guarantee the best results use the freshest available vegetables.

Stuffed Parsleyed Onions

Although devised as a vegetarian dish, these stuffed onions make a wonderful accompaniment to meat dishes, or an appetizing supper dish with crusty bread and a salad.

INGREDIENTS

4 large onions
4 tablespoons cooked rice
4 teaspoons finely chopped fresh
parsley, plus extra to garnish
4 tablespoons finely grated
sharp Cheddar cheese
salt and pepper
2 tablespoons olive oil
1 tablespoon white wine, to moisten

Serves 4

1

Cut a slice from the top of each onion and scoop out the center to leave a thick shell.

2

Combine all the remaining ingredients, moistening with enough wine to mix well. Preheat the oven to 350°F.

3

Fill the onions and bake for 45 minutes. Serve garnished with parsley.

Stuffed Tomatoes with Wild Rice, Corn and Cilantro

These tomatoes could be served as a light meal or as an accompaniment for meat or fish.

INGREDIENTS

8 medium tomatoes
¼ cup corn kernels
2 tablespoons white wine
¼ cup cooked wild rice
1 clove garlic
¼ cup grated Cheddar cheese
1 tablespoon chopped fresh cilantro
salt and pepper
1 tablespoon olive oil

Serves 4

1

Cut the tops off the tomatoes and remove the seeds with a small spoon. Scoop out all the flesh and chop finely—remember to chop the tops as well.

2

Preheat the oven to 350°F. Put the chopped tomato in a pan. Add the corn and the white wine. Cover with a close-fitting lid and simmer until tender. Drain the excess liquid.

3

Combine all the remaining ingredients except the olive oil, adding salt and pepper to taste. Carefully spoon the mixture into the tomatoes, piling it higher in the center. Sprinkle the oil over the top, arrange the tomatoes in an ovenproof dish and bake at 350°F for 15–20 minutes, until cooked through.

Garden Salad

You can use any fresh, edible flowers from your garden for this beautiful salad.

INGREDIENTS

1 Romaine lettuce
6 oz arugula
1 small frisée lettuce
fresh chervil and tarragon sprigs
1 tbsp chopped fresh chives
handful of mixed edible flower
heads, such as nasturtiums
or marigolds

For the dressing
3 tbsp olive oil
1 tbsp white-wine vinegar
½ tsp French mustard
1 garlic clove, crushed
pinch of sugar

Serves 4

1

Mix the Romaine, arugula and frisée leaves
and herbs together.

2

Make the dressing by whisking all the
ingredients together in a large bowl. Toss the
salad leaves in the bowl with the dressing,
add the flower heads and serve at once.

Creamy Layered Potatoes

Cook the potatoes on top of the stove first to help the dish to bake more quickly.

INGREDIENTS

*3–3½ lb large potatoes, peeled
and sliced
2 large onions, sliced
6 tbsp unsalted butter
1¼ cups heavy cream
salt and freshly ground
black pepper*

Serves 6

___1___

Preheat the oven to 400°F. Blanch the sliced
potatoes for 2 minutes, and drain well.

___2___

Place the potatoes, onions, butter and cream
in a pan, stir well and cook for about
15 minutes. Transfer to a large ovenproof
dish, season well and bake for 1 hour, until
the potatoes are tender.

New Potato Salad

Potatoes freshly dug up from the garden are the best. Always leave the skins on: just wash the dirt away thoroughly. If you add the mayonnaise and other ingredients when the potatoes are hot, the flavors will develop as the potatoes cool.

INGREDIENTS

2 lb baby new potatoes
2 green apples, cored and chopped
4 scallions, chopped
3 celery stalks, finely chopped
2/3 cup homemade or storebought
mayonnaise
salt and freshly ground
black pepper

Serves 6

1

Cook the potatoes in salted, boiling water for about 20 minutes, or until they are very tender.

2

Drain the potatoes well and immediately add the remaining ingredients and stir until well mixed. Let cool and serve cold.

Green Bean Salad

The secret of this recipe is to dress the beans while still hot.

INGREDIENTS

6 oz cherry tomatoes,
halved
1 tsp sugar
1 lb green beans, topped
and tailed
6 oz feta cheese, cubed
salt and freshly ground
black pepper

For the dressing
6 tbsp olive oil
3 tbsp white-wine vinegar
1/4 tsp Dijon mustard
2 garlic cloves, crushed
salt and freshly ground
black pepper

Serves 6

1

Preheat the oven to 450°F. Put the cherry tomatoes on a baking sheet and sprinkle the sugar, salt and pepper over. Roast for 10 minutes, then let cool. Meanwhile, cook the beans in boiling salted water for 10 minutes.

2

Make the dressing by whisking together the oil, vinegar, mustard, garlic and seasoning. Drain the beans and immediately pour the vinaigrette over and mix well. When cool, stir in the roasted tomatoes and the feta cheese. Serve chilled.

Rosemary Roast Potatoes

These unusual roast potatoes use far less fat than conventional ones, and because they still have their skins they have more flavor, too.

INGREDIENTS

2¼ pounds small red potatoes
2 teaspoons walnut or sunflower oil
2 tablespoons fresh rosemary leaves
salt and paprika

Serves 4

NOTE
This preparation is also delicious with tiny new potatoes, especially if you roast them with chunks of red onion.

1
Preheat the oven to 475°F. Scrub the potatoes. If they are large, cut them in half. Place in a pan of cold water and bring to a boil. Drain.

2
Drizzle the oil over the potatoes and shake the pan to coat them evenly.

3
Put the potatoes in a shallow roasting pan. Sprinkle with the rosemary, salt and paprika. Roast for 30–45 minutes. Serve hot.

Baked Zucchini in Tomato Sauce

Zucchini and tomatoes have a natural affinity. Use fresh tomatoes, cooked and puréed, instead of canned, if possible.

INGREDIENTS

1 teaspoon olive oil
3 large zucchini, thinly sliced
½ small red onion, finely chopped
1¼ cups puréed tomatoes
2 tablespoons chopped fresh thyme
garlic salt and freshly ground black pepper
fresh thyme sprigs, to garnish

Serves 4

1
Preheat the oven to 375°F. Brush a baking dish with olive oil. Arrange half the zucchini and onion in the dish.

2
Spoon half the tomatoes over the vegetables. Sprinkle with some of the fresh thyme, then season to taste with garlic salt and pepper. Repeat with the remaining ingredients. Cover the dish and bake for 40–45 minutes. Garnish with thyme sprigs and serve hot.

Spicy Fried Potatoes

Give fried potatoes a hint of heat by tossing them with spiced vinegar.
Sliced peppers add a splash of color.

INGREDIENTS

2 garlic cloves, sliced
½ teaspoon crushed chilies
½ teaspoon ground cumin
2 teaspoons paprika
2 tablespoons red or white wine
vinegar
1½ pounds small new potatoes
5 tablespoons olive oil
1 red or green bell pepper, seeded and
sliced
coarse sea salt, to serve (optional)

Serves 4

1

Mix the garlic, chilies and cumin in a
mortar. Crush with a pestle, then stir in the
paprika and wine vinegar.

2

Bring a saucepan of lightly salted water to
a boil and cook the potatoes, in their skins,
for about 15 minutes, until almost tender.
Drain, peel, if preferred, and cut into
chunks. Heat the oil in a large frying pan;
sauté the potatoes until golden.

3

Add the spiced garlic mixture to the
potatoes with the sliced pepper and
continue to cook, stirring, for 2 minutes.
Serve warm or at room temperature. Scatter
with coarse sea salt, if desired, to serve.

Turnip Greens with Parmesan and Garlic

Farmhouse cooks know how to turn everyday ingredients into treats. Here, turnip greens are flavored with onions, garlic and Parmesan cheese. They do not need long cooking, because the leaves are quite tender.

INGREDIENTS

3 tablespoons olive oil
2 garlic cloves, crushed
4 scallions, sliced
12 ounces turnip greens, thinly sliced,
tough stalks removed
1/4 cup water
2/3 cup grated Parmesan cheese
salt and freshly ground black pepper
shavings of Parmesan cheese, to
garnish

Serves 4

1

Heat the olive oil in a large saucepan and stir-fry the garlic and scallions for 2 minutes. Add the turnip greens and stir-fry for 2–3 minutes, so that the greens are coated in oil. Add the water.

2

Bring to a boil, lower the heat, cover and simmer, stirring frequently, until the greens are tender. Bring the liquid to a boil again, allow the excess to evaporate, then stir in the Parmesan and seasoning. Serve at once with extra shavings of cheese.

Spiced Turnips with Spinach and Tomatoes

Sweet baby turnips, tender spinach and ripe tomatoes make tempting partners in this simple vegetable stew.

INGREDIENTS

1 pound fresh, ripe tomatoes
4 tablespoons olive oil
2 onions, chopped or sliced
1 pound baby turnips, peeled
1 teaspoon paprika
¼ cup water
½ teaspoon sugar
¼ cup chopped fresh cilantro
1 pound fresh baby spinach, well rinsed, stems removed
salt and freshly ground black pepper

Serves 6

1

Plunge the tomatoes into a bowl of boiling water for 30 seconds, then refresh in a bowl of cold water. Peel away the tomato skins and chop roughly.

2

Heat the olive oil in a large frying pan and fry the onion for about 5 minutes, until golden. Add the baby turnips, tomatoes, paprika and water to the pan and cook until the tomatoes are pulpy. Cover and continue cooking until the baby turnips are soft.

3

Stir in the sugar and cilantro, then add the spinach and a little salt and pepper and cook for another 2–3 minutes, until the spinach has wilted. Serve warm or at room temperature.

Salsify and Spinach Casserole

The spinach in this recipe adds color and makes it go further. However, if you have plenty of salsify, plus the patience to peel it, increase the quantity and leave out the spinach.

INGREDIENTS

juice of 2 lemons
1 pound salsify
1 pound fresh spinach leaves, well rinsed
²⁄₃ cup chicken or vegetable stock
1¼ cups light cream or half-and-half
salt and freshly ground black pepper

Serves 4

____
2

Meanwhile, cook the spinach in a large saucepan over medium heat for 2–3 minutes, shaking the pan occasionally, until the leaves have wilted. Place the stock, cream and seasoning in a small saucepan and heat through very gently, stirring.

____
3

Grease a baking dish generously with butter. Drain the salsify and spinach and arrange in layers in the prepared dish. Pour the stock and cream mixture over the vegetables and bake for about 1 hour, until the top is golden brown and bubbling.

____
1

Preheat the oven to 325°F. Add a quarter of the lemon juice to a large bowl of water. Trim and peel the salsify. Place each peeled root immediately in the lemon water, to prevent discoloration. Bring a saucepan of water to a boil. Add the remaining lemon juice. Cut the salsify into 2-inch lengths, add it to the pan and simmer for about 10 minutes, until just tender.

Glazed Carrots with Cider

Cooking young carrots with the minimum of liquid brings out the best of their flavor, while the cider adds a pleasant sharpness.

INGREDIENTS

1 pound young carrots
2 tablespoons butter
1 tablespoon brown sugar
½ cup cider
¼ cup vegetable stock
1 teaspoon Dijon mustard
1 tablespoon finely chopped fresh
parsley

Serves 4

NOTE

If the carrots are cooked before the liquid in the saucepan has reduced, transfer the carrots to a serving dish and rapidly boil the liquid until thick. Pour the liquid over the carrots and sprinkle with parsley.

1

Trim the tops and bottoms of the carrots. Peel or scrape them. Using a sharp knife, cut them into short thin sticks. Melt the butter in a frying pan and sauté the carrots for 4–5 minutes.

2

Sprinkle on the sugar and cook, stirring, for 1 minute. Add the cider and stock, bring to a boil and stir in the mustard. Partially cover the pan and simmer for 10–12 minutes, until the carrots are just tender. Remove the lid and continue cooking until the liquid has reduced to a thick sauce. Toss the carrots with the parsley and spoon into a warmed serving dish.

Carrot, Apple and Orange Coleslaw

This dish is as delicious as it is easy to make. The garlic and herb dressing adds the necessary contrast to the sweetness of the salad.

INGREDIENTS ·

12 ounces young carrots, finely grated
2 apples
1 tablespoon lemon juice
1 large orange, peeled and segmented

For the dressing
3 tablespoons olive oil
¼ cup sunflower oil
3 tablespoons lemon juice
1 garlic clove, crushed
¼ cup plain yogurt
1 tablespoon chopped mixed fresh herbs
salt and freshly ground black pepper

Serves 4

1

Place the carrots in a large serving bowl. Quarter the apples, remove the core from each wedge and then slice thinly. Sprinkle the apples with lemon juice to prevent discoloration, then add to the carrots, with the orange segments.

2

To make the dressing, place the oils, lemon juice and garlic in a jar with a tight-fitting lid and shake vigorously. Add the remaining ingredients and shake again. Just before serving, pour the dressing over the salad and toss well.

Brussels Sprouts with Chestnuts

A traditional Christmas speciality, this combination of crisp, tender Brussels sprouts and chestnuts is perennially popular.

8 ounces chestnuts
½ cup milk
4 cups small tender Brussels sprouts, trimmed
2 tablespoons butter
1 shallot, finely chopped
2–3 tablespoons dry white wine or water

Serves 4–6

1

Cut a cross in the bottom of each chestnut. Bring a saucepan of water to a boil, drop in the chestnuts and boil for 6–8 minutes. Peel while still warm, then return to the clean pan. Add the milk and enough water to cover the chestnuts. Simmer for 12–15 minutes. Drain and set aside.

2

Remove any wilted or yellow leaves from the Brussels sprouts. Trim the root end but leave intact or the leaves will separate. Using a small knife, cut a cross in the bottom of each sprout.

3

Melt the butter in a large, heavy frying pan, and cook the shallot for 1–2 minutes, until just softened. Add the Brussels sprouts and wine or water. Cover and cook over medium heat for 6–8 minutes, shaking the pan occasionally and adding a little more water if necessary.

4

Add the poached chestnuts and toss gently, then cover and cook for 3–5 minutes more. Serve immediately.

Leeks in Egg and Lemon Sauce

Tender young leeks, picked fresh from the vegetable garden, cooked and cooled in a tart, creamy sauce, taste absolutely superb.

INGREDIENTS

1½ pounds baby leeks, trimmed, slit and washed
1 tablespoon cornstarch
2 teaspoons sugar
2 egg yolks
juice of 1½ lemons
salt

Serves 4

___3___

Whisk the egg yolks with the lemon juice and stir gradually into the cooled sauce. Cook over very low heat, stirring constantly, until the sauce is fairly thick. Immediately remove from the heat and continue stirring for 1 minute. Taste and add salt or sugar as necessary. Cool slightly.

___4___

Pour the sauce over the leeks. Cover and chill for at least 2 hours before serving.

NOTE
Do not let the sauce overheat after adding the egg yolks or it may curdle.

___1___

Lay the leeks flat in a large saucepan, cover with water and add a little salt. Bring to a boil, lower the heat, cover and simmer for 4–5 minutes, until just tender.

___2___

Lift out the leeks, drain well and arrange in a shallow serving dish. Mix 1 cup of the cooking liquid with the cornstarch in a saucepan. Bring to a boil, stirring constantly, then cook until the sauce thickens slightly. Stir in the sugar. Cool slightly.

Peas with Lettuce and Onion

Shelling peas is a traditional pastime in the farmhouse kitchen. Sweet young peas taste delicious when cooked with strips of lettuce.

INGREDIENTS

*1 tablespoon butter
1 small onion, finely chopped
1 small Boston lettuce, halved and
sliced into thin strips
3½ cups shelled fresh peas (from
about 3½ pounds pods), or
thawed frozen peas
3 tablespoons water
salt and freshly ground black pepper*

Serves 4–6

1

Melt the butter in a heavy saucepan. Add
the onion and cook over medium-low heat
for about 3 minutes, until just softened.
Place the lettuce strips on top of the onion
and add the peas and water. Season lightly
with salt and pepper.

2

Cover the pan tightly and cook the lettuce
and peas over low heat until the peas are
tender—fresh peas will take 10–20
minutes, frozen peas about 10 minutes.
Toss lightly and serve at once.

Fava Beans with Cream

Skinned fava beans are a beautiful bright green. Try this simple way of serving them.

INGREDIENTS

*1 pound shelled fava beans (from
about 4½ pounds pods)
6 tablespoons crème fraîche or
whipping cream
salt and freshly ground black pepper
finely snipped chives, to garnish*

Serves 4–6

1

Bring a large pan of lightly salted water to
a boil and add the beans. Reduce the heat
slightly and cook the beans for about
8 minutes, until just tender. Drain, refresh
under cold running water, then drain again.

2

Remove the skins by slitting each bean and
gently squeezing out the kernel.

NOTE
If you can find them, fresh flageolet or lima
beans can be served in the same way.

3

Put the skinned beans in a saucepan with
the cream and seasoning, cover and heat
through gently. Sprinkle with the snipped
chives and serve at once.

Baked Beans with Sage

Sage is a somewhat neglected herb, used for stuffings and liver dishes, but little else. It gives baked beans an incomparable flavor.

INGREDIENTS

3¼ cups dried beans, such as
cannellini
¼ cup olive oil
2 garlic cloves, crushed
3 fresh sage leaves
1 leek, finely sliced
1 can (14 ounces) chopped tomatoes
salt and freshly ground black pepper

Serves 6–8

1

Carefully pick over the beans, discarding any stones or other particles. Place the beans in a bowl and cover with water. Soak for at least 6 hours, or overnight. Drain.

2

Preheat the oven to 350°F. Heat the oil in a small saucepan and sauté the garlic cloves and sage leaves for 3–4 minutes. Remove from the heat.

3

Put the beans in a large, deep baking dish and add the leek and tomatoes. Stir in the garlic and sage with the oil. Add enough fresh water to cover the beans by 1 inch. Mix well. Cover the dish and bake for 1¾ hours.

4

Remove the dish from the oven, stir the beans, and season with salt and pepper. Return the dish to the oven, uncovered, and cook the beans for 15 minutes more, or until tender. Remove from the oven and allow to stand for 7–8 minutes before serving.

Squash à la Greque

A traditional French-style dish that is usually made with mushrooms.
Make sure that you cook the baby squash until they are quite tender,
so they can fully absorb the delicious flavors of the marinade.

INGREDIENTS

6 oz pattypan squash
1 cup white wine
juice of 2 lemons
fresh thyme sprig
bay leaf
small bunch of fresh chervil,
coarsely chopped
¼ tsp coriander seeds, crushed
¼ tsp black peppercorns, crushed
5 tbsp olive oil

Serves 4

1

Blanch the pattypan squash in boiling
water for 3 minutes, and then refresh them
in cold water.

2

Place all the remaining ingredients in a pan,
add ⅔ cup of water and simmer for 10
minutes, covered. Add the patty pans and
cook for 10 minutes. Remove with a slotted
spoon when they are cooked and tender
to the bite.

3

Reduce the liquid by boiling hard for
10 minutes. Strain it and pour it over the
squashes. Leave until cool for the flavors to
be absorbed. Serve cold.

Eggplants with Garlic and Tomato Glaze

An unusual way of cooking eggplants, which tend to absorb large amounts of oil when fried. Roasting the slices in the oven makes them slightly crisp.

INGREDIENTS

2 eggplants, about 8 ounces each, sliced
2 garlic cloves, crushed
3 tablespoons tomato paste
6–8 tablespoons olive oil
½ teaspoon sugar
salt and freshly ground black pepper
chopped flat leaf parsley, to garnish

Serves 2–4

1

Spread out the eggplants on paper towels. Sprinkle them with salt and leave for about 30 minutes. Meanwhile, preheat the oven to 375°F. Mix the garlic and tomato paste with 1 tablespoon of the oil in a bowl. Add the sugar, salt and pepper.

2

Rinse, drain and dry the eggplant slices. Pour about ¼ cup of the oil into a baking pan and arrange the eggplant slices in a single layer. Spoon a little of the garlic-tomato mixture over each one. Drizzle with the remaining oil, then bake for about 30 minutes. Arrange on a flat dish, garnish with chopped parsley and serve.

Beets with Sour Cream

Freshly picked from the farmhouse garden, small beets make a delicious snack or side dish when simply boiled and served with sour cream.

INGREDIENTS

1 pound small uncooked beets
1¼ cups chilled sour cream
salt and freshly ground black pepper
fresh dill sprigs, to garnish

Serves 4

NOTE
To prepare the beets, cut off the leaves about 1 inch from the tops and remove the thin roots. Wash the beets very well, removing any dirt with a vegetable brush. Take care not to cut them or the color will leach out.

1

Put the beets in a saucepan with water to cover generously. Season well, bring to a boil and simmer for 30–40 minutes. Drain the beets, and while they are still warm, use a knife to peel off the skin.

2

Spoon the chilled sour cream onto individual plates. Cut the beets into wedges and use one to make a pretty pink swirl. Arrange the wedges around the plates and garnish with dill sprigs.

Globe Artichokes with Green Beans and Aïoli

Gloriously garlicky aïoli is the perfect partner for freshly cooked vegetables.

INGREDIENTS

8 ounces green beans
3 small globe artichokes
1 tablespoon olive oil
pared rind of 1 lemon
coarse salt for sprinkling
lemon wedges, to garnish

For the aïoli
6 large garlic cloves
2 teaspoons white wine vinegar
1 cup olive oil
salt and freshly ground black pepper

Serves 4–6

NOTE
If you prefer to make the aïoli by hand, crush the garlic with the vinegar, then gradually whisk in the oil.

1

Make the aïoli. Crush the garlic with the flat blade of a chef's knife. Put it in a blender and add the vinegar. Blend to a paste. With the machine switched on, gradually pour in the olive oil through the feed-tube until the mixture is thick and smooth. Season with salt and pepper to taste.

2

Cook the beans in a large saucepan of lightly salted boiling water for 1–2 minutes, until they have softened slightly. Remove from the water with a slotted spoon and set aside. Trim the artichoke stalks close to the bottom. Add the artichokes to the pan of boiling water and cook for about 30 minutes or until you can easily pull away a leaf from the base. Drain well.

3

Using a sharp knife, cut the artichokes in half lengthwise and ease out the choke using a teaspoon. Arrange the artichokes and beans on serving plates and drizzle with the oil. Scatter with the lemon rind and season with coarse salt and a little pepper. Spoon the aïoli into the artichoke hearts and serve warm, garnished with the lemon wedges.

Stewed Artichokes

*There are lots of wonderful ways to serve artichokes. Try them lightly
stewed with garlic, parsley and wine.*

INGREDIENTS

*1 lemon
4 large or 6 small globe artichokes
2 tablespoons butter
¼ cup olive oil
2 garlic cloves, finely chopped
¼ cup chopped fresh parsley
3 tablespoons water
6 tablespoons milk
6 tablespoons white wine
salt and freshly ground black pepper*

Serves 6

_____
2

_____
3

_____
1

Squeeze the lemon juice into a large bowl of
cold water. Wash the artichokes and prepare
them one at a time. Cut off only the tip
from the stem. Peel the stem, pulling off
the small leaves around it, and continue
until you reach the taller inner leaves.

Slice off the topmost part of the leaves. Cut
the artichoke into four or six segments,
then cut out the bristly choke from each
segment. Place the artichokes in the lemon
water to prevent discoloration. Bring a
large pan of water to a boil and blanch the
artichokes for 4–5 minutes. Drain well.

Heat the butter and olive oil in a large
saucepan and fry the garlic and parsley for
2–3 minutes. Stir in the artichokes, water
and milk, season, then cook for 10 minutes,
or until the liquid has evaporated. Stir in
the wine, cover and cook until the
artichokes are tender. Serve hot or at
room temperature.

Green Beans with Tomatoes

Green beans in a rich tomato sauce make a dish that is as colorful as it is good to eat.

INGREDIENTS

*3 tablespoons olive oil
1 onion, preferably red, very finely
sliced
12 ounces plum tomatoes, peeled and
finely chopped
½ cup water
5–6 fresh basil leaves, torn into shreds
1 pound fresh green beans, trimmed
salt and freshly ground black pepper*

Serves 4–6

_____
1

_____
2

Heat the oil in a large frying pan. Add the
onion slices and cook for 5–6 minutes,
until just soft. Add the tomatoes and cook
over medium heat for 6–8 minutes, until
they soften. Stir in the water. Season with
salt and pepper, and add the basil.

Stir in the beans, turning them in the pan
to coat them with the sauce. Cover the pan,
and cook over medium heat for 15–20
minutes, until tender. Stir occasionally, and
add a little more water if the sauce dries
out too much. Serve hot or cold.

Leek and Onion Tart

This unusual recipe isn't a normal tart with pastry, but an all-in-one savory
slice that is excellent served as an accompaniment to roast meat.

INGREDIENTS

4 tbsp unsalted butter
12 oz leeks, sliced thinly
2 cups self-rising flour
½ cup Crisco
⅔ cup water
salt and freshly ground
black pepper

Serves 4

1

Preheat the oven to 400°F. Melt the butter
in a pan and sauté the leeks until soft.
Season well.

2

Mix the flour, fat and water together in a
bowl to make a soft but sticky dough.
Mix into the leek mixture in the pan. Place
in a greased shallow ovenproof dish and bake
for 30 minutes, or until brown and crispy.
Serve sliced, as a vegetable accompaniment.

Braised Red Cabbage

The combination of red wine vinegar and sugar gives this dish a sweet, yet tart, flavor. In France it is often served with game, but it is also delicious with pork, duck or cold meats.

INGREDIENTS

2 tablespoons vegetable oil
2 onions, thinly sliced
2 apples, peeled, cored and thinly sliced
1 head red cabbage (about 2 pounds), trimmed, cored, halved and thinly sliced
¼ cup red wine vinegar
1–2 tablespoons sugar
¼ teaspoon ground cloves
1–2 teaspoons mustard seeds
⅓ cup raisins or currants
about ½ cup red wine or water
1–2 tablespoons red currant jelly
salt and freshly ground black pepper

Serves 6–8

1

Heat the oil in a large stainless-steel saucepan over medium heat. Fry the onions for 7–10 minutes, until golden. Stir in the apples and cook, stirring, for 2–3 minutes, until they are just softened.

2

Add the cabbage, red wine vinegar, sugar, cloves, mustard seeds, raisins or currants, red wine or water and salt and pepper, stirring until well mixed. Bring to a boil, stirring occasionally.

3

Cover and cook over fairly low heat for 35–40 minutes, stirring occasionally, until the cabbage is tender and the liquid is just absorbed. Add a little more red wine or water if the pan boils dry before the cabbage is tender. Just before serving, stir in the red currant jelly to sweeten and glaze the cabbage.

Eggs and Cheese

Baskets of eggs and wheels of cheese invite experimentation. These simple ingredients form the basis of a wide range of delicious dishes, most of which can be made in moments. Use free-range eggs and farmhouse cheeses for the best possible flavor. The following section shows just how versatile and appetizing eggs and cheese are. The recipes themselves are all fairly straightforward, but the end results are positively mouthwatering.

Carrot and Cilantro Soufflés

Use tender young carrots for this light-as-air dish.

1 lb carrots
2 tbsp fresh chopped
cilantro
4 eggs, separated
salt and freshly ground
black pepper

Serves 4

1

Peel the carrots.

2

Cook in boiling salted water for 20 minutes
or until tender. Drain, and process until
smooth in a food processor.

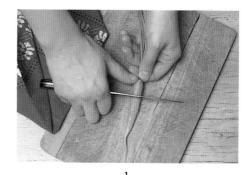

3

Preheat the oven to 400°F. Season the
puréed carrots well, and stir in the chopped
cilantro.

4

Fold the egg yolks into the carrot mixture.

5

In a separate bowl, whisk the egg whites
until stiff.

6

Fold the egg whites into the carrot mixture
and pour into four greased ramekins. Bake
for about 20 minutes or until risen
and golden. Serve immediately.

Mediterranean Quiche

The strong Mediterranean flavors of tomatoes, peppers and anchovies beautifully complement the cheese pastry in this unusual quiche.

INGREDIENTS

For the pastry
2 cups all-purpose flour
pinch of salt
pinch of mustard
½ cup butter, chilled and
cubed
2 oz Gruyère cheese, grated

For the filling
2 oz can of anchovies in oil,
drained
¼ cup milk
2 tbsp French mustard
3 tbsp olive oil
2 large Spanish onions, peeled
and sliced
1 red bell pepper, seeded and
very finely sliced
3 egg yolks
1½ cups heavy cream
1 garlic clove, crushed
6 oz sharp Cheddar
cheese, grated
2 large tomatoes, thickly sliced
salt and freshly ground
black pepper
2 tbsp chopped fresh basil,
to garnish

Serves 8

1

First make the pastry. Place the flour, salt and mustard in a food processor, add the butter and process the mixture until it resembles bread crumbs.

2

Add the cheese and process again briefly. Add enough iced water to make a stiff dough: it will be ready when the dough forms a ball. Wrap with plastic wrap and chill for 30 minutes.

3

Meanwhile, make the filling. Soak the anchovies in the milk for 20 minutes. Pour off the milk.

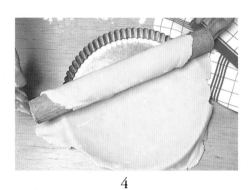

4

Roll out the chilled pastry and line a 9 in loose-based quiche pan. Spread the mustard over and chill for a further 15 minutes.

5

Preheat the oven to 400°F. Heat the oil in a frying pan and cook the onions and red pepper until soft. In a separate bowl, beat the egg yolks, cream, garlic and Cheddar cheese together; season well. Arrange the tomatoes in a single layer in the pastry crust. Top with the onion and pepper mixture and the anchovy fillets. Pour the egg mixture over. Bake for 30–35 minutes. Sprinkle over the basil and serve.

Cheese and Bacon Quiche

Quiches are great country fare, ideal for al fresco meals. To pack for a picnic, double wrap the pan in foil and support it in a sturdy box.

INGREDIENTS

*12 ounces unsweetened pastry, thawed
if frozen
1 tablespoon Dijon mustard
6 lean bacon strips, chopped
3 eggs
1½ cups light cream or half-and-half
1 onion, chopped
5 ounces Gruyère cheese, diced
salt and freshly ground black pepper
fresh parsley, to garnish*

Serves 6–8

1

Preheat the oven to 400°F. Roll out the pastry and line a 9-inch pie pan. Prick the bottom of the pastry shell and bake for 15 minutes. Brush the shell with mustard and bake for 5 minutes more. Reduce the oven temperature to 350°F.

2

Fry the bacon until crisp and browned. Beat the eggs and cream, season with salt and pepper and set aside.

3

Drain the bacon. Pour off most of the fat from the pan, add the onion and cook gently for about 15 minutes.

4

Sprinkle half the cheese over the pastry, then the onion, followed by the bacon and remaining cheese. Pour in the egg mixture and bake for 35–45 minutes, until set. Serve warm, garnished with parsley.

Swiss Chard Omelet

This flat omelet can also be made with fresh spinach, but the large leaves of Swiss chard—a member of the beet family—are more traditional.

INGREDIENTS

1½ pounds Swiss chard leaves, without stems
¼ cup olive oil
1 large onion, sliced
5 eggs
salt and freshly ground black pepper
fresh parsley sprig, to garnish

Serves 6

___3___

Beat the eggs in a large bowl. Season with salt and pepper, then stir in the cooked vegetables. Heat the remaining oil in a large frying pan, pour in the egg mixture and reduce the heat to medium-low. Cook the omelet, covered, for 5–7 minutes, until the egg mixture is set around the edges and almost set on top.

___4___

To turn the omelet over, loosen the edges and slide it onto a large plate. Place the frying pan upside down over the omelet and, holding both tightly, carefully invert pan and plate. Cook the omelet for another 2–3 minutes. Slide the omelet onto a serving plate and serve hot or at room temperature, garnished with parsley.

___1___

Wash the chard well in several changes of water and pat dry. Stack four or five leaves at a time and slice across into thin ribbons. Steam the chard until wilted, then drain in a sieve and press out any liquid with the back of a spoon.

___2___

Heat half the olive oil in a large frying pan. Add the onion and cook over medium-low heat for about 10 minutes, stirring occasionally, until soft. Add the chard and cook for another 2–4 minutes, until the leaves are tender.

Omelet with Herbs

Sometimes the simplest dishes are the most satisfying. Fresh farm eggs, sour cream and herbs make a speedy but superb meal.

INGREDIENTS

2 eggs
1 tablespoon butter
1 tablespoon crème fraîche or sour cream
1 teaspoon chopped fresh mixed herbs (such as tarragon, chives, parsley or marjoram)
salt and freshly ground black pepper

Serves 1

VARIATIONS
Other omelet fillings could include sautéed sliced mushrooms, diced ham or crumbled crisp bacon, creamed spinach or thick tomato sauce and grated cheese.

1

Beat the eggs and salt and pepper in a bowl. Melt the butter in an omelet pan until foamy, then pour in the eggs. When the mixture starts to set on the bottom of the pan, lift up the sides with a spatula and tilt the pan to allow the uncooked egg to run underneath.

2

When the omelet is set, but still soft on top, spoon the crème fraîche or sour cream over the center and sprinkle with the herbs. Hold the pan over a warmed plate. With a spatula, lift one edge of the omelet and fold it over the middle. Tilt the pan so that the omelet folds into thirds and slide it out onto the plate.

Egg-stuffed Tomatoes

Effective, but surprisingly easy to prepare, this is the perfect dish for a quick lunch. For the most enjoyable result, eat immediately.

INGREDIENTS

¾ cup mayonnaise
2 tablespoons snipped fresh chives
2 tablespoons torn fresh basil leaves
2 tablespoons chopped fresh parsley
4 ripe tomatoes
4 hard-cooked eggs, sliced
salt
lettuce leaves, to serve

Serves 4

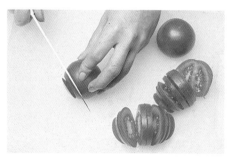

1

Mix the mayonnaise and herbs in a small bowl and set aside. Place the tomatoes core-end down and make deep cuts to within ½-inch of the bottom. (There should be the same number of cuts in each tomato as there are slices of egg.)

2

Fan open the tomatoes and sprinkle with salt, then insert an egg slice into each slit. Place each stuffed tomato on a plate with lettuce leaves and serve with the herb mayonnaise.

Baked Cheese Polenta with Tomato Sauce

Polenta, or cornmeal, is a staple food in Italy. Cooked, cut into shapes when set, then baked with a tomato sauce, it makes a delicious meal.

4 cups water
1 teaspoon salt
2¼ cups instant polenta
1 teaspoon paprika
½ teaspoon grated nutmeg
2 tablespoons olive oil
1 large onion, finely chopped
2 garlic cloves, crushed
2 pounds tomatoes, peeled and chopped
or 2 cans (14 ounces each) chopped
tomatoes
1 tablespoon tomato paste
1 teaspoon sugar
3 ounces Gruyère cheese, grated
salt and freshly ground black pepper

Serves 4

1

Preheat the oven to 400°F. Line an
11 x 7-inch baking pan with plastic wrap.
Bring the water to a boil with the salt,
pour in the polenta in a steady stream and
cook, stirring constantly, for 5 minutes, or
until it forms a thick mass. Beat in the
paprika and nutmeg, then pour into the
prepared pan and smooth the surface.
Let cool and set.

2

Heat the oil in a large, shallow pan and
cook the onion and garlic until soft. Stir in
the tomatoes, tomato paste and sugar, with
salt and pepper to taste. Bring to a boil,
lower the heat and simmer for 20 minutes.

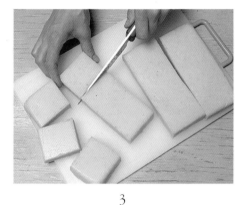

3

Turn out the polenta onto a chopping board
and cut into 2-inch squares. Place half the
squares in a greased baking dish. Spoon half
the tomato sauce on top, and sprinkle with
half the cheese. Repeat the layers. Bake for
about 25 minutes, until
a golden color.

Tortellini with Cream, Butter and Cheese

Pasta provides the perfect quick meal. The cream sauce takes only minutes to prepare, and tastes wonderful.

INGREDIENTS

*4 cups fresh tortellini
4 tablespoons (½ stick) butter, plus extra for greasing
1¼ cups heavy cream
4-ounce piece fresh Parmesan cheese
freshly grated nutmeg
salt and freshly ground black pepper
fresh herbs, to garnish*

Serves 4–6

NOTE
Feel free to try different cheeses, but don't use light cream because it will curdle.

3

Grate the Parmesan and stir ¾ cup into the sauce until melted. Season the sauce with salt, pepper and nutmeg. Preheat the broiler.

4

Drain the pasta and spoon it into the serving dish. Pour the sauce on top, sprinkle with the remaining cheese and broil until brown. Garnish and serve immediately.

1

Cook the pasta in a large saucepan of boiling salted water according to the manufacturer's instructions. Butter a flameproof serving dish.

2

Meanwhile, melt the butter in a medium saucepan and stir in the cream. Bring to a boil and cook for 2–3 minutes, until slightly thickened.

Cauliflower with Cheese Sauce

This dish is equally good made with broccoli. Serve it with bacon for a special treat.

INGREDIENTS

*1 pound cauliflower, broken into
florets
3 tablespoons butter
6 tablespoons all-purpose flour
1½ cups milk
1 bay leaf
pinch of grated nutmeg
1 tablespoon Dijon mustard
1½ cups grated Gruyère or Emmenthal
cheese
salt and freshly ground black pepper*

Serves 4–6

1

Preheat the oven to 350°F. Lightly butter a
large gratin pan or shallow baking dish.

2

Bring a large saucepan of salted water to a
boil, add the cauliflower florets and cook
for 6–8 minutes, until just tender.

3

Melt the butter in a heavy saucepan over
medium heat, add the flour and cook until
just golden, stirring occasionally. Gradually
add the milk, stirring constantly until the
sauce boils and thickens. Add the bay leaf
and salt, pepper and nutmeg. Add the
mustard. Reduce the heat and simmer for
5 minutes, stirring occasionally, then
remove the bay leaf. Stir in half the cheese.

4

Arrange the cauliflower in the pan.
Pour the cheese sauce on top and sprinkle
with the remaining cheese. Bake for about
20 minutes, until bubbly and
well browned.

Poached Eggs with Spinach

When the vegetable garden yields fresh spinach, serve this simple dish.

INGREDIENTS

2 tablespoons butter
1 pound baby spinach leaves, well rinsed
½ teaspoon vinegar
4 eggs
salt and freshly ground black pepper

For the hollandaise sauce
2 egg yolks
1 tablespoon lemon juice
1 tablespoon water
12 tablespoons (1½ sticks) butter
salt and white pepper

Serves 4

NOTE
For a well-shaped poached egg, swirl the water whirlpool-fashion before slipping the egg into the center.

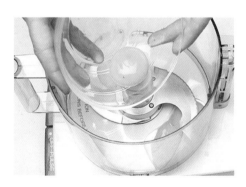

1

Make the hollandaise sauce. Mix the egg yolks, lemon juice and water in a food processor. Melt the butter in a small pan until foaming. With the machine running, slowly pour the hot butter into the processor in a thin stream. Season the thickened sauce with more lemon juice if needed and salt and pepper. Transfer the sauce to a bowl, cover and keep warm.

2

Melt the butter in a heavy frying pan over a medium heat. Add the spinach and cook until wilted, stirring occasionally. Season and keep warm.

3

Bring a pan of lightly salted water to a boil and add the vinegar. Break an egg into a saucer and slide the egg into the water. Reduce the heat and simmer for a few minutes until the white is set and the yolk is still soft. Remove with a slotted spoon and drain. Trim any untidy edges with scissors and keep the poached egg warm. Poach the remaining eggs in the same way.

4

To serve, spoon the spinach onto warmed plates and make a hollow in each mound. Place the eggs on top and pour a little hollandaise sauce on top.

Eggs in Pepper Nests

Pepper strips look pretty and provide an interesting nest for baked eggs topped with cream.

INGREDIENTS

2 red bell peppers
1 green bell pepper
2 tablespoons olive oil
1 large onion, finely sliced
2 garlic cloves, crushed
5–6 tomatoes, skinned and chopped
½ cup tomato juice
generous pinch of dried basil
4 eggs
8 teaspoons light cream or
half-and-half
pinch of cayenne pepper (optional)
salt and freshly ground black pepper

Serves 4

1

Preheat the oven to 350°F. Seed and thinly slice the bell peppers. Heat the olive oil in a large frying pan. Sauté the onion and garlic gently for about 5 minutes, stirring, until softened.

2

Add the bell peppers to the onion and sauté for 10 minutes. Stir in the tomatoes and juice, the basil and seasoning. Cook gently for 10 minutes more, until the peppers are soft.

3

Spoon the mixture into four ovenproof dishes. Make a well in the center of each and break in an egg. Spoon 2 teaspoons cream over the yolk of each egg and sprinkle with a little black pepper or cayenne. Bake for 12–15 minutes, until the white of the egg is lightly set. Serve immediately with crusty bread.

Eggs Baked in Ham and Potato Hash

4 tablespoons (¹/₂ stick) butter
1 large onion, chopped
12 ounces cooked ham, diced
1 pound cooked potatoes, diced
1 cup grated Cheddar cheese
2 tablespoons ketchup
2 tablespoons Worcestershire sauce
6 eggs
few drops of Tabasco sauce
salt and freshly ground black pepper
chopped fresh parsley, to garnish

Serves 6

3

Make six wells in the hash. Break each egg
in turn into a small bowl or saucer and slip
into one of the wells.

4

Melt the remaining butter. Season with
Tabasco sauce, then dribble the seasoned
butter over the eggs and hash. Bake for
15–20 minutes or until the eggs are set.
Garnish with parsley and serve.

1

Preheat the oven to 325°F. Melt half the
butter in a frying pan. Cook the onion until
soft, stirring occasionally, then place it in a
bowl and stir in the ham, potatoes, cheese,
ketchup and Worcestershire sauce.

2

Season the mixture and spread it in a
buttered baking dish in a layer about
1 inch deep. Bake for 10 minutes.

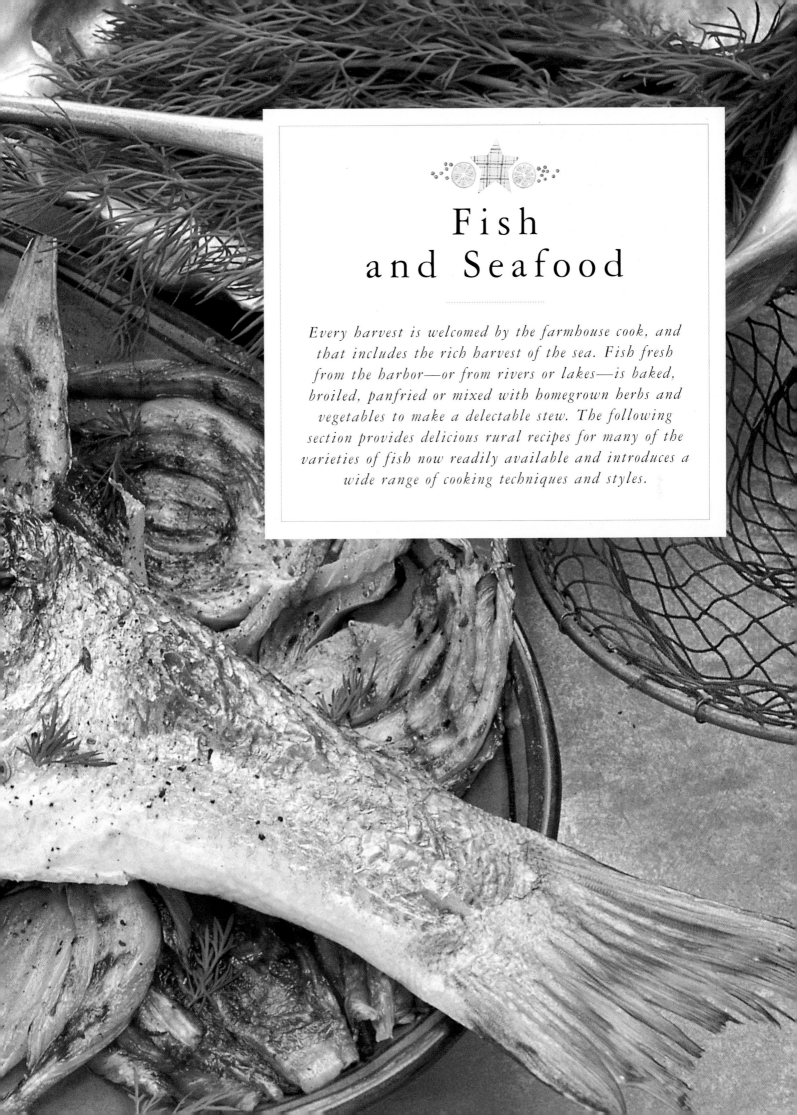

Fish
and Seafood

Every harvest is welcomed by the farmhouse cook, and that includes the rich harvest of the sea. Fish fresh from the harbor—or from rivers or lakes—is baked, broiled, panfried or mixed with homegrown herbs and vegetables to make a delectable stew. The following section provides delicious rural recipes for many of the varieties of fish now readily available and introduces a wide range of cooking techniques and styles.

Mackerel with Roasted Blueberries

Fresh blueberries burst with flavor when roasted, and their sharpness complements the rich flesh of mackerel very well.

INGREDIENTS

2 tsp all-purpose flour
4 small cooked, smoked mackerel
4 tbsp unsalted butter
juice of ½ lemon
salt and freshly ground
black pepper

For the roasted blueberries
1 lb blueberries
2 tbsp superfine sugar
1 tbsp unsalted butter
salt and freshly ground
black pepper

Serves 4

1

Preheat the oven to 400°F. Season the flour. Dip each fish fillet into the flour to coat it well.

2

Dot the butter on the fillets and bake in the oven for 20 minutes.

3

Place the blueberries, sugar, butter and seasoning in a separate small roasting pan and roast them, basting them occasionally, for 15 minutes. To serve, drizzle the lemon juice over the roasted mackerel, accompanied by the roasted blueberries.

Chunky Seafood Stew

There's no more pleasant a way of spending an evening than sitting around the scrubbed farmhouse table and tucking into an excellent seafood stew.

INGREDIENTS

3 tablespoons olive oil
2 large onions, chopped
1 green bell pepper, seeded and sliced
3 carrots, chopped
3 garlic cloves, crushed
2 tablespoons tomato paste
2 cans (14 ounces each) chopped tomatoes
3 tablespoons chopped fresh parsley
1 teaspoon chopped fresh thyme
1 tablespoon shredded fresh basil leaves
$\frac{1}{2}$ cup dry white wine
1 pound shrimp, peeled and deveined, or cooked peeled shrimp
3–3$\frac{1}{2}$ pounds mussels or clams (in shells), or a mixture, thoroughly cleaned
2 pounds halibut or other firm, white fish fillets, cut into 2-inch chunks
1$\frac{1}{2}$ cups fish stock or water
salt and freshly ground black pepper
extra chopped fresh herbs, to garnish

Serves 6

2

Stir in the tomato paste, canned tomatoes, herbs and wine. Bring to a boil, lower the heat and simmer for 20 minutes. Add the shrimp, mussels and/or clams, fish pieces and stock or water. Season with salt and pepper to taste.

3

Bring back to a boil, then simmer for 5–6 minutes, until the shrimp turn pink, the fish flakes easily and the mussels and clams open. If using cooked shrimp, add them for the last 2 minutes only. Serve in large soup plates, garnished with chopped herbs.

1

Heat the oil in a flameproof casserole. Add the onions, green bell pepper, carrots and garlic and cook for about 5 minutes, until tender.

Cod, Basil and Tomato with a Potato Thatch

With a green salad, this makes an ideal dish for lunch or a family supper.

INGREDIENTS

2 pounds smoked cod
2½ cups white cod
5 cups milk
2 sprigs basil
1 sprig lemon thyme
10 tablespoons butter
1 onion, peeled and chopped
¾ cup flour
2 tablespoons tomato paste
2 tablespoons chopped basil
12 medium-size old potatoes
1⅓ cups milk
salt and pepper
1 tablespoon chopped parsley

Serves 8

1

Place both kinds of fish in a roasting pan with the milk, 5 cups water and herbs. Simmer for 3–4 minutes. Let cool in the liquid for about 20 minutes. Drain the fish, reserving the liquid for use in the sauce. Flake the fish, taking care to remove any skin and bone, which should be discarded.

2

Melt 6 tablespoons butter in a pan, add the onion and cook for about 4 minutes, until tender but not browned. Add the flour, tomato paste and half the basil. Gradually add the reserved fish stock, adding a little more milk if necessary to make a fairly thin sauce. Bring this to a boil, season with salt and pepper, and add the remaining basil. Add the fish carefully and stir gently. Transfer to an ovenproof dish.

3

Preheat the oven to 350°F. Boil the potatoes until tender. Add the remaining 4 tablespoons butter and the milk, and mash well. Add salt and pepper to taste and cover the fish, using a fork to create a pattern. If you like, you can freeze the pie at this stage. Bake for 30 minutes. Serve with chopped parsley.

Broiled Sea Bass with Fennel

Fennel has an unmistakable flavor and goes particularly well with fish.

INGREDIENTS

1 sea bass, 4–4½ pounds, cleaned
4–6 tablespoons olive oil
2–3 teaspoons fennel seeds
2 large fennel bulbs, with fronds attached
¼ cup Pernod
salt and freshly ground black pepper

Serves 6–8

___

1

With a sharp knife, make three or four deep cuts in both sides of the fish. Brush the fish with olive oil and season with salt and pepper. Sprinkle the fennel seeds in the stomach cavity and in the cuts. Set aside while you cook the fennel.

___

2

Preheat the broiler. Trim the fennel fronds and quarter the bulbs lengthwise. Remove the core and slice thinly. Reserve the fennel fronds. Put the fennel slices on the broiler rack and brush with oil. Broil for 4 minutes on each side, until tender. Transfer to a large dish or platter.

___

3

Place the fish on the oiled broiler pan and position about 5 inches from the heat. Broil for 10–12 minutes on each side, brushing occasionally with oil. Transfer the fish to the platter on top of the fennel. Garnish with the fennel fronds. Heat the Pernod in a small pan, light it and pour it, flaming, over the fish. Serve immediately.

Herbed Halibut Mille-feuille

The herbs add their own special flavors to the creamy fish.

INGREDIENTS

9 ounces puff pastry
butter for baking sheet
1 egg, beaten
1 small onion
1 tablespoon fresh ginger, grated
½ tablespoon oil
⅔ cup fish stock
1 tablespoon dry sherry
3 halibut, cooked and flaked
8 ounces crabmeat
salt and pepper
1 avocado
juice of 1 lime
1 mango
1 tablespoon chopped mixed parsley,
thyme and chives, to garnish

Serves 2

1

Roll the pastry out into a 10-inch square, trim the edges and place on a buttered baking sheet. Prick with a fork, then let it rest in the refrigerator for at least 30 minutes. Preheat the oven to 450°F. Brush the top of the pastry with beaten egg and bake for 10–15 minutes or until golden.

3

Fry the onion and ginger in the oil until tender. Add the fish stock and sherry, and simmer for 5 minutes. Add the halibut and crabmeat, and season to taste. Peel and chop the avocado and toss with the lime juice. Peel and chop the mango, reserving a few slices for garnishing. Add the avocado and the mango to the fish.

2

Let the pastry cool for a few minutes, then cut it twice across in one direction and once in the other to make six pieces. Let cool completely.

4

Build up alternate layers of fish and pastry, starting and finishing with a piece of pastry. Serve garnished with herbs and mango slices.

Salmon and Ginger Pie

This exceptional pie is highly recommended. The recipe uses salmon's special flavor to the full.

INGREDIENTS

1¾ pounds middle cut of salmon
3 tablespoons walnut oil
1 tablespoon lime juice
2 teaspoons chopped fresh lemon thyme
2 tablespoons white wine
salt and pepper
14 ounces puff pastry
¼ cup slivered almonds
3–4 pieces preserved ginger in syrup,
chopped
1 egg, beaten

Serves 4–6

1

Split the salmon in half, remove all the bones and skin and divide into 4 fillets. Mix the oil, lime juice, thyme, wine and pepper, and pour over the fish. Let marinate overnight in the refrigerator.

3

Divide the pastry into 2 pieces, one slightly larger than the other, and roll out—the smaller piece should be large enough to accommodate 2 of the salmon fillets and the second piece 2 inches larger all around.

2

Drain the fillets. Discard the marinade. Preheat the oven to 375°F. Place 2 of the fillets on the smaller piece of pastry, and season. Add the almonds and ginger and cover with the other 2 fillets.

4

Season again, cover with the second piece of pastry and seal well. Brush with beaten egg and decorate with any leftover pastry. Bake for 40 minutes.

Leek and Monkfish with Thyme Sauce

Monkfish is a well-known fish now, thanks to its excellent flavor and firm texture.

INGREDIENTS

2 pounds monkfish, cubed
salt and pepper
12 tablespoons butter
4 leeks, sliced
1 tablespoon flour
⅔ cup fish or
vegetable stock
2 teaspoons finely chopped fresh thyme,
plus more to garnish
juice of 1 lemon
⅔ cup light cream
radicchio, to garnish

Serves 4

1

Season the fish to taste. Melt about a third of the butter in a pan, and fry the fish for a short time. Set aside.

2

Fry the leeks in the pan with another third of the butter until they have softened. Set aside with the fish.

3

In a saucepan, melt the rest of the butter. Add the butter from the pan, stir in the flour, and add the stock. As the sauce thickens, add the thyme and lemon juice.

4

Return the leeks and monkfish to the pan and cook gently for a few minutes. Add the cream and season to taste. Serve immediately, garnished with thyme and radicchio leaves.

Fish Stew with Calvados, Parsley and Dill

This rustic stew harbors all sorts of interesting flavors and will please and intrigue. Many varieties of fish can be used, just choose the freshest and best.

INGREDIENTS

*2 pounds assorted white fish
1 tablespoon chopped parsley, plus a few leaves to garnish
8 ounces mushrooms
1 can (8 ounces) tomatoes
salt and pepper
2 teaspoons flour
1 tablespoon butter
2 cups cider
3 tablespoons Calvados
1 large bunch fresh dill sprigs, reserving 4 fronds to garnish*

Serves 4

1

Chop the fish roughly and place it in a casserole or stewing pot with the parsley, mushrooms and tomatoes, adding salt and pepper to taste.

2

Preheat the oven to 350°F. Work the flour into the butter. Heat the cider and stir in the flour and butter mixture a little at a time. Cook, stirring, until it has thickened slightly.

3

Add the cider mixture and the remaining ingredients to the fish and mix gently. Cover and bake for about 30 minutes. Serve garnished with sprigs of dill and parsley leaves.

Pan-fried Trout with Bacon

This dish can also be cooked under the broiler.

INGREDIENTS

*1 tbsp all-purpose flour
4 trout, cleaned and gutted
3 oz lean bacon
4 tbsp butter
1 tbsp olive oil
juice of ½ lemon
salt and freshly ground
black pepper*

Serves 4

1

Pat the trout dry with paper towels and
mix the flour and seasoning together.

2

Roll the trout in the seasoned flour mixture
and wrap tightly in the bacon. Heat a
heavy frying pan. Heat the butter and
oil in the pan and fry the trout for 5 minutes
on each side. Serve immediately, with the
lemon juice drizzled on top.

Trout Fillets with Spinach and Mushroom Sauce

Portobello mushrooms form the basis of this rich sauce, served with trout that has been filleted to make it easier to eat.

INGREDIENTS

4 brown or rainbow trout, filleted and skinned to make 8 fillets

For the spinach and mushroom sauce
6 tablespoons butter
¼ medium onion, chopped
8 ounces portobello mushrooms, chopped
1¼ cups boiling chicken stock
1 package (8 ounces) frozen chopped spinach
2 teaspoons cornstarch, mixed to a paste with 1 tablespoon cold water
⅔ cup crème fraîche
grated nutmeg
salt and freshly ground black pepper

Serves 4

NOTE
Spinach and mushroom sauce is also good with fillets of cod, haddock and sole.

2

Stir the cornstarch paste into the mushroom mixture. Bring to a boil, then simmer gently to thicken. Purée the mixture. Add the crème fraîche and season with salt, pepper and nutmeg. Blend briefly, then scrape into a serving bowl and keep warm.

3

Melt the remaining butter in a large nonstick frying pan. Season the trout and cook for 6 minutes, or until thoroughly cooked, turning once. Serve with the sauce either poured on top or served separately. New potatoes and baby corn would be ideal accompaniments.

1

To make the sauce, melt 4 tablespoons of the butter in a frying pan and sauté the onion until soft. Add the mushrooms and cook until the juices begin to run. Stir in the stock and the spinach and cook until the spinach has thawed completely.

Trout with Almonds

This quick and easy recipe can be cooked for four, adapted by cooking the trout in two frying pans or in batches.

INGREDIENTS

2 trout, about 12 ounces each, cleaned
6 tablespoons all-purpose flour
4 tablespoons (½ stick) butter
¼ cup slivered or sliced almonds
2 tablespoons dry white wine
salt and freshly ground black pepper

Serves 2

NOTE

The easiest way to coat the trout is to put the flour in a large plastic bag and season with salt and pepper. Place the trout, one at a time, in the bag and shake until evenly coated. Shake off the excess flour from the fish.

1

Coat the trout in the flour, seasoned with salt and pepper. Melt half the butter in a large frying pan. When it is foamy, add the trout and cook for 6–7 minutes on each side, until the skin is golden brown and the flesh next to the bone is opaque. Transfer the fish to warmed plates and keep hot.

2

Add the remaining butter to the pan and cook the almonds until just lightly browned. Add the wine to the pan and boil for 1 minute, stirring constantly, until slightly syrupy. Pour or spoon over the fish and serve immediately.

Tuna with Garlic, Tomatoes and Herbs

In France, where this recipe originated, dried herbs are used, but fresh herbs are fine.

INGREDIENTS

4 tuna steaks, about 1 inch thick
(6–7 ounces each)
2–3 tablespoons olive oil
3 or 4 garlic cloves, finely chopped
¼ cup dry white wine
3 ripe tomatoes, skinned, seeded and chopped
1–2 tablespoons dried mixed herbs
salt and freshly ground black pepper
fresh basil leaves, to garnish

Serves 4

NOTE

Tuna is often served pink in the middle. If you prefer it cooked through, reduce the heat and cook for a few extra minutes.

1

Season the tuna steaks with salt and pepper. Set a heavy frying pan over high heat. When very hot, add the oil and swirl to coat. Add the tuna steaks and press down gently, then reduce the heat to medium and cook for 6–8 minutes, turning once, until just slightly pink in the center.

2

Transfer the steaks to a serving plate and keep hot. Add the garlic to the pan and fry for 15–20 seconds, then pour in the wine and boil until reduced by half. Add the tomatoes and herbs and cook for 2–3 minutes. Season with pepper and pour over the fish steaks. Serve, garnished with fresh basil leaves.

Pan-fried Garlic Sardines

Lightly fry a sliced clove of garlic to garnish the fish. This dish could also be made with small mackerel or fresh anchovies if available.

INGREDIENTS

8 fresh sardines
2 tablespoons olive oil
4 garlic cloves
finely grated rind of 2 lemons
2 tablespoons chopped fresh parsley
salt and freshly ground black pepper

For the tomato bread
2 large ripe beefsteak tomatoes
8 slices crusty bread, toasted

Serves 4

1

Gut and clean the sardines. Pat them dry with paper towels.

2

Heat the oil in a frying pan and cook the garlic cloves until soft.

3

Remove the garlic from the pan, then sauté the sardines for 4–5 minutes. Sprinkle with the lemon rind, parsley and seasoning.

4

Cut the tomatoes in half and rub them on the toast. Discard the skins. Serve each sardine on a slice of the tomato toast.

Stuffed Sardines

Adding a savory golden raisin and pine nut stuffing takes sardines into a sophisticated league.

INGREDIENTS

8 fresh sardines
2 tablespoons olive oil
1½ cups bread crumbs
⅓ cup golden raisins
⅔ cup pine nuts
1 can (2 ounces) anchovy fillets,
drained
¼ cup chopped fresh parsley
1 onion, finely chopped
salt and freshly ground black pepper
lemon wedges, to garnish

Serves 4

1

Preheat the oven to 400°F. Gut and clean the sardines; dry with paper towels. Heat the oil in a frying pan and fry the bread crumbs until golden.

2

Add the golden raisins, pine nuts, anchovies, parsley, onion and seasoning to the bread crumbs.

3

Stuff each sardine with the mixture. Close the fish firmly and closely pack together in a single layer in an ovenproof dish.

4

Scatter any remaining filling over the sardines and drizzle with olive oil. Bake for 30 minutes and serve with lemon wedges.

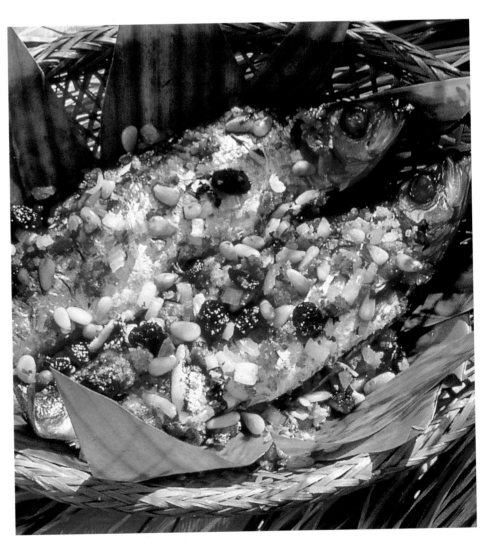

Baked Cod, Greek-style

Cod is often served with little preparation. Although it can be delicious in its simplest form, it sometimes deserves more sophisticated treatment. In this recipe, the fish is baked with onions and tomatoes.

INGREDIENTS

1¼ cups olive oil
2 onions, thinly sliced
3 large ripe tomatoes, roughly chopped
3 garlic cloves, thinly sliced
1 teaspoon sugar
1 teaspoon chopped fresh dill
1 teaspoon chopped fresh mint
1 teaspoon chopped fresh celery leaves
1 tablespoon chopped fresh parsley

1¼ cups water
6 cod steaks (6–8 ounces each)
juice of 1 lemon
salt and freshly ground black pepper
extra dill, mint or parsley, to garnish

Serves 6

1

Heat the oil in a large, shallow pan and cook the onions until pale golden. Stir in the tomatoes, garlic, sugar, dill, mint, celery leaves and parsley. Pour in the water. Season with salt and pepper, then simmer, uncovered, for 25 minutes, until the liquid has reduced by one-third.

2

Add the cod steaks and cook gently for 10–12 minutes, until the fish is just cooked. Remove from the heat and pour the lemon juice over the fish. Cover and let stand for about 20 minutes before serving. Arrange the cod in a dish and spoon the sauce over the top. Garnish with herbs and serve warm or at room temperature.

Cod with Lentils and Leeks

This unusual dish is great for entertaining. The vegetables can be cooked ahead of time and the fish baked while the first course is served.

INGREDIENTS

1 cup green lentils, rinsed
1 bay leaf
1 garlic clove, finely chopped
grated zest of 1 orange
grated zest of 1 lemon
pinch of ground cumin
1 tablespoon butter
1 pound leeks, thinly sliced
1¼ cups whipping cream
1 tablespoon lemon juice, or to taste
1¾-pound thick cod or haddock fillet, skinned
salt and freshly ground black pepper

Serves 4

1

Put the lentils, bay leaf and garlic in a large saucepan and add enough water to cover by 1 inch. Bring to a boil, boil gently for 10 minutes, then reduce the heat and simmer for 15–30 minutes more, until the lentils are just tender.

2

Drain the lentils and discard the bay leaf, then stir in half the orange zest and all the lemon zest. Season with the ground cumin and salt and pepper. Transfer to a shallow baking dish or gratin dish. Preheat the oven to 375°F.

3

Melt the butter over medium heat in a saucepan, add the leeks and cook gently, stirring frequently, until just softened. Add 1 cup of the cream and the remaining orange zest and cook gently for 15–20 minutes, until the leeks have softened completely and the cream has thickened slightly. Stir in the lemon juice and season with salt and plenty of pepper.

4

Cut the fish into four pieces and remove any remaining bones. Season the fish with salt and pepper, place the pieces on top of the lentil mixture and press down slightly. Cover each piece of fish with a quarter of the leek mixture and divide the remaining ¼ cup cream among them. Bake for about 30 minutes, until the fish is cooked thoroughly and the topping is golden.

Special Seafood Stew

Not all farmhouse cooking is plain and pastoral—on special occasions family and friends will celebrate with a special dish, like this classic seafood stew from Spain.

INGREDIENTS

1 cooked lobster
24 fresh mussels
1 large monkfish tail
1 tablespoon all-purpose flour
8 ounces squid, cut into rings
6 tablespoons olive oil
12 large shrimp

1 pound ripe tomatoes
2 large mild onions
4 garlic cloves, crushed
2 tablespoons brandy
2 bay leaves
1 teaspoon paprika
1 red chili, seeded and chopped

1¼ cups fish stock
3 tablespoons ground almonds
2 tablespoons chopped fresh parsley
salt and freshly ground black pepper

Serves 6

1

Cut the lobster in half and remove the dark intestine that runs down the length of the tail. Crack the claws using a hammer. Scrub the mussels, discarding any that are damaged and any open ones that do not close when tapped with a knife. Cut the monkfish fillets away from the central cartilage; cut each fillet into three pieces.

2

Season the flour and toss the monkfish and squid in it. Heat the oil in a frying pan. Add the monkfish and squid and fry quickly; remove from the pan. Fry the shrimp, then remove from the pan. Plunge the tomatoes into boiling water for 30 seconds, then refresh in cold water. Peel away the skins and chop roughly.

3

Chop the onions and add to the pan with three of the garlic cloves. Fry for 3 minutes, then add the brandy and light it. When the flames die down, add the tomatoes, bay leaves, paprika, chili and stock. Bring to a boil, reduce the heat and simmer for 5 minutes.

4

Add the mussels, cover and cook for 3–4 minutes, until the shells have opened. Remove the mussels from the sauce and discard any that remain closed. Arrange all the fish, including the lobster, in a large flameproof serving dish.

5

Blend the ground almonds to a paste with the remaining garlic clove and parsley and stir into the sauce. Season with salt and pepper. Pour the sauce over the fish and lobster and cook gently for about 5 minutes, until hot. Serve immediately with a green salad and plenty of warmed bread.

Seafood Risotto

Risotto is the perfect example of a rustic dish that can be adapted to take advantage of whatever is in season. This seafood version varies, depending on the current catch.

INGREDIENTS

*¼ cup sunflower oil
1 onion, chopped
2 garlic cloves, crushed
1 cup arborio rice
7 tablespoons white wine
6 cups hot fish stock
12 ounces mixed seafood, such as
shrimp, mussels, squid, cut into rings,
or clams, prepared according to type
grated zest of ½ lemon
2 tablespoons tomato paste
1 tablespoon chopped fresh parsley
salt and freshly ground black pepper*

Serves 4

1

Heat the oil in a heavy saucepan and gently sauté the onion and garlic until soft. Add the rice and stir to coat the grains with oil. Pour in the wine and stir over medium heat until it has been absorbed.

2

Ladle in ⅔ cup of the hot stock and cook, stirring constantly, until the liquid is absorbed by the rice. Continue stirring and adding stock in similar quantities, until half is left. This should take about 10 minutes.

3

Stir in the seafood and cook for 2–3 minutes. Add the remaining stock as before, until the rice is cooked. It should be quite creamy and the grains just tender. Stir in the lemon rind, tomato paste and parsley. Season with salt and pepper and serve warm.

Italian Shrimp Skewers

These are delicious, whether broiled or cooked on the grill, and would be ideal for a summer party.

INGREDIENTS

*2 pounds jumbo shrimp, peeled
¼ cup olive oil
3 tablespoons vegetable oil
1¼ cups very fine dry bread crumbs
1 garlic clove, crushed
1 tablespoon chopped fresh parsley
salt and freshly ground black pepper
lemon wedges, to serve*

Serves 4

1

Slit the shrimp down their backs and remove the dark veins. Rinse in cold water and pat dry. Mix the oils in a large bowl and add the shrimp, turning them in the oil to coat evenly.

2

Add the bread crumbs, garlic and parsley to the bowl, with salt and pepper to taste. Toss the oiled shrimp in the mixture to coat them evenly. Cover and let marinate for 1 hour.

3

Preheat the broiler or outdoor grill. Thread the shrimp onto four metal skewers, curling them up as you do so, so that the tail is skewered in the middle. Place the skewers in the broiler pan or on the grill and cook for about 2 minutes on each side, until the bread crumbs are golden. Serve with lemon wedges.

Crab Cakes

These crab cakes are full of flavor thanks to mustard, horseradish and Worcestershire sauce.

INGREDIENTS

1 pound fresh lump crabmeat
1 egg, well beaten
1 teaspoon Dijon mustard
2 teaspoons prepared horseradish
2 teaspoons Worcestershire sauce
8 scallions, finely chopped
3 tablespoons chopped fresh parsley
1½ cups fresh bread crumbs
1 tablespoon whipping cream
(optional)
1 cup dry bread crumbs
3 tablespoons butter
salt and freshly ground black pepper
lemon wedges and fresh dill sprigs, for
serving

Serves 3–6

1

In a mixing bowl, combine the crabmeat, egg, mustard, horseradish, Worcestershire sauce, scallions, parsley and fresh bread crumbs. Mix gently, leaving the pieces of crabmeat as large as possible. Season to taste. If the mixture is too dry to hold together, add the cream. Divide the crab mixture into six portions and shape into round, flat cakes.

2

Spread out the dry bread crumbs on a plate. Coat the crab cakes on both sides. Melt the butter in a frying pan. Fry the crab cakes for about 3 minutes on each side, or until golden. Add more fat if necessary. Serve with lemon wedges and dill.

Baked Stuffed Crab

Good cooking means meals that are good-looking as well as tasty. This recipe scores on both counts.

INGREDIENTS

4 freshly cooked crabs
1 celery stalk, diced
1 scallion, finely chopped
1 small fresh green chili, seeded and
finely chopped
5 tablespoons mayonnaise
2 tablespoons fresh lemon juice
1 tablespoon snipped fresh chives
½ cup fresh bread crumbs
½ cup grated Cheddar cheese
2 tablespoons butter, melted
salt and freshly ground black pepper
fresh parsley sprigs, to garnish

Serves 4

1

Preheat the oven to 375°F. Remove the meat from the crab body and claws. Reserve the whole shells.

2

Scrub the crab shells. Cut open the seam on the underside with scissors. The inner part of the shell should break off cleanly along the seam. Rinse the shells and dry them well.

3

In a bowl, combine the crabmeat, celery, scallion, chili, mayonnaise, lemon juice and chives. Season and mix. In a separate bowl, toss together the bread crumbs, cheese and melted butter.

4

Pile the crab mixture into the shells. Sprinkle with the cheese mixture. Bake for about 20 minutes, until golden brown. Serve hot, garnished with parsley.

Poultry
and Game

Chicken and duck play a prominent role in farmhouse cooking, with slow-cooked casseroles, hearty pies and handsome roasts filling the kitchen with tempting aromas. Game birds and venison are valued in their season, and country cooks know just how delicious rabbit can be. The following pages are full of delicious recipes that will be particularly enjoyed as the main meal of the day.

Traditional Chicken Pot Pie

With its golden crust and rich chicken and vegetable filling, an old-fashioned chicken pot pie is a favorite family dish.

INGREDIENTS

4 tablespoons (½ stick) butter
1 onion, chopped
3 carrots, diced
1 parsnip, diced
3 tablespoons all-purpose flour
1½ cups chicken stock
5 tablespoons medium sherry
5 tablespoons dry white wine
¾ cup whipping cream
¾ cup frozen peas, thawed
12 ounces cooked chicken meat, in chunks
1 teaspoon dried thyme

1 tablespoon finely chopped fresh parsley
salt and freshly ground black pepper
1 egg, beaten with 2 tablespoons milk, to glaze

For the pastry
1½ cups all-purpose flour
½ teaspoon salt
½ cup vegetable shortening
2–3 tablespoons ice water

Serves 6

1

For the pastry, sift the flour and salt into a mixing bowl. Rub in the shortening until the mixture resembles coarse bread crumbs, then add enough ice water to form a dough. Dust with flour, wrap and chill.

2

Preheat the oven to 400°F. Heat half the butter in a saucepan. Add the onion, carrots and parsnip and cook for 10 minutes, until softened. Remove from the pan with a slotted spoon.

3

Melt the remaining butter in the pan. Add the flour and cook for 2 minutes, stirring constantly. Stir in the stock, sherry and white wine. Bring the sauce to a boil and cook for 1 minute, stirring constantly.

4

Stir the cream, peas, chicken, thyme and parsley into the sauce. Season to taste with salt and pepper. Simmer for 1 minute, stirring, then transfer the mixture to an 8-cup pie dish.

5

On a lightly floured surface, roll out the pastry to a ½-inch thickness. Cover the pie and trim off the excess pastry. Dampen the rim of the dish. With a fork, press the pastry to the rim to seal. Cut decorative shapes from the pastry trimmings.

6

Brush the pastry all over with the egg glaze. Arrange the pastry shapes on top, then brush again with the egg glaze. Make one or two holes in the crust so steam can escape during baking. Bake the pie for about 35 minutes, until the pastry is golden brown. Serve hot.

Chicken and Corn Stew

Serve this rustic stew with biscuits; the combination works remarkably well.

INGREDIENTS

4 pounds chicken, cut into serving pieces
paprika
2 tablespoons olive oil
2 tablespoons butter
1 pound onions, chopped
1 green or yellow bell pepper, cored,
seeded and chopped
1 can (14 ounces) chopped tomatoes
1 cup white wine
2 cups chicken stock or water
3 tablespoons chopped fresh parsley
½ teaspoon Tabasco sauce
1 tablespoon Worcestershire sauce
2 cups corn kernels (fresh, frozen, or
drained canned)
1 cup fava beans (fresh or frozen)
3 tablespoons all-purpose flour
salt and freshly ground black pepper
Italian parsley sprigs, to garnish

Serves 6

1

Rinse the chicken pieces under cool water and pat dry with paper towels. Sprinkle each piece lightly with salt and paprika.

2

Heat the oil and butter in a large, heavy saucepan. Add the chicken pieces and fry until golden brown on all sides. Remove with tongs and set aside.

3

Reduce the heat to low and cook the onions and pepper for 8–10 minutes, until softened. Stir in the tomatoes, wine, stock or water, parsley and sauces. Turn up the heat and bring to a boil.

4

Return the chicken to the pan, pushing it down in the sauce. Cover, reduce the heat and simmer for 30 minutes, stirring occasionally.

5

Add the corn and beans and mix well. Partly cover and cook for 30 minutes more. Skim off or blot any surface fat.

6

Mix the flour with a little water to make a paste. Gradually add ¾ cup of the hot liquid from the pan. Stir this mixture into the stew and season with salt and pepper. Cook for 5–8 minutes more, stirring occasionally. Garnish and serve.

Chicken and Mushroom Cobbler

There's something very comforting about a cobbler, with its biscuit topping and satisfying filling. Adding wild mushrooms enriches the flavor, but button mushrooms are fine for a family meal.

INGREDIENTS

¼ *cup vegetable oil*
1 *onion, chopped*
1 *celery stalk, sliced*
1 *small carrot, peeled and diced*
3 *skinless, boneless chicken breasts*
4 *cups mixed fresh mushrooms and wild mushrooms, sliced*
6 *tablespoons all-purpose flour*
2¼ *cups hot chicken stock*
2 *teaspoons Dijon mustard*
2 *tablespoons medium sherry*
2 *teaspoons wine vinegar*
salt and freshly ground black pepper

For the cobbler topping
2½ *cups self-rising flour*
pinch of celery salt
pinch of cayenne pepper
½ *cup butter, diced*
½ *cup grated Cheddar cheese*
⅔ *cup cold water*
1 *beaten egg, to glaze*

Serves 4

1

Preheat the oven to 400°F. Heat the oil in a large, heavy saucepan and fry the onion, celery and carrot gently for 8–10 minutes, to soften without coloring. Add the cubed chicken and cook briefly. Add the mushrooms, cook until the juices run, then stir in the flour.

2

Remove the pan from the heat and gradually stir in the stock. Return the pan to the heat and simmer gently to thicken, stirring constantly. Stir in the mustard, sherry, vinegar and seasoning.

3

To make the topping, sift the flour, celery salt and cayenne into a bowl or food processor fitted with a metal blade. Rub in the butter and half the cheese until the mixture resembles coarse bread crumbs. Add the water and combine without overmixing.

4

Turn out the dough onto a floured board, form it into a round and flatten to a thickness of about ½ inch. Cut out as many 2-inch rounds as you can, using a plain cutter.

5

Transfer the chicken mixture to a 5-cup pie dish, then overlap the topping rounds around the edge. Brush with beaten egg, scatter with the remaining cheese and bake for 25–30 minutes, until the topping has risen well and is golden.

Chicken with Sloe Gin and Juniper

Juniper is used in the manufacture of gin, and this dish is flavored with
both sloe gin and juniper. Sloe gin is easy to make and has a wonderful flavor,
but it can also be bought ready-made.

INGREDIENTS

2 tablespoons butter
2 tablespoons sunflower oil
8 chicken breast fillets
12 ounces carrots, cooked
1 clove garlic, peeled and crushed
1 tablespoon finely chopped parsley
¼ cup chicken stock
¼ cup red wine
¼ cup sloe gin
1 teaspoon crushed juniper berries
salt and pepper
1 bunch basil, to garnish

Serves 8

1

Melt the butter with the oil in a pan, and
sauté the chicken fillets until they are
browned on all sides.

2

In a food processor, combine all the
remaining ingredients except the basil,
and blend to a smooth puree. If the
mixture seems too thick, add a little more
red wine or water until a thinner
consistency is reached.

3

Put the chicken breasts in a pan, pour the
sauce over the top and cook until the
chicken is cooked through, which should
take about 15 minutes. Adjust the
seasoning and serve garnished with
chopped fresh basil leaves.

Turkey with Apples and Bay Leaves

*Apples from the orchard combine with bay leaves and Madeira to create
a delicious turkey casserole with a handsome garnish.*

INGREDIENTS

6 tablespoons butter
*1½ pounds turkey breast fillets, cut
into ¾-inch slices*
4 tart apples, peeled and sliced
3 bay leaves
6 tablespoons Madeira
⅔ cup chicken stock
2 teaspoons cornstarch
⅔ cup heavy cream
salt and freshly ground black pepper

Serves 4

1

Preheat the oven to 350°F. Melt
2 tablespoons of the butter in a large,
shallow pan and sear the turkey breast
fillets until sealed on all sides. Transfer to a
casserole and add 2 more tablespoons butter
and half the apple slices and cook gently
for 1–2 minutes.

2

Tuck the bay leaves around the turkey
breasts. Stir in ¼ cup of the Madeira and
all the stock. Simmer for 3–4 minutes, then
pour the apple mixture over the turkey
in the casserole. Cover and bake for
40 minutes.

3

Mix the cornstarch to a paste with a little
of the cream, then stir in the rest of the
cream. Add this mixture to the casserole,
season, stir well, then return to the oven for
10 minutes to allow the sauce to thicken.

4

To make the garnish, melt the remaining
butter in a frying pan and gently sauté the
remaining apple slices until just tender.
Add the remaining Madeira and light it.
Once the flames have died down, continue
to cook the apple slices until they are
lightly browned. Arrange them on top of
the turkey mixture.

Roast Turkey with Mushroom Stuffing

A fresh farm turkey tastes wonderful with a wild mushroom stuffing.
Serve it with a wild mushroom gravy for maximum impact.

INGREDIENTS

10–12-pound free-range turkey
butter, for basting
watercress, to garnish

For the mushroom stuffing
4 tablespoons (½ stick) butter
1 onion, chopped
8 ounces wild mushrooms, chopped
1½ cups fresh white bread crumbs
4 ounces pork sausages, skinned
1 small fresh truffle, sliced (optional)
5 drops truffle oil (optional)
salt and freshly ground black pepper

For the gravy
5 tablespoons medium sherry
1⅔ cups chicken stock
4 teaspoons cornstarch
1 teaspoon Dijon mustard
2 teaspoons water
½ teaspoon red wine vinegar
pat of butter

Serves 6–8

1

Preheat the oven to 425°F. To make the stuffing, melt the butter in a saucepan and sauté the onion gently without coloring. Add the mushrooms and stir until their juices begin to flow. Transfer from the pan to a bowl and add all the remaining ingredients, including the truffle and truffle oil, if using. Season and stir well to combine.

2

Spoon the stuffing into the neck cavity of the turkey and enclose, fastening the skin on the underside with a skewer.

3

Rub the skin of the turkey with butter, place in a large roasting pan and roast for 50 minutes. Lower the temperature to 350°F and cook for 2½ hours more.

4

Transfer the turkey to a carving board, cover loosely with foil and keep hot. To make the gravy, spoon off the fat from the roasting juices, then place the pan over medium heat until the juices are reduced to a sediment. Stir in the sherry, then stir in the chicken stock.

5

Place the cornstarch and mustard in a small bowl. Stir in the water and wine vinegar. Stir this mixture into the juices in the roasting pan and simmer to thicken. Season and stir in a pat of butter. Garnish the turkey with watercress. Pour the gravy into a gravy boat and serve separately.

Cassoulet

If ever there was a dish that exemplifies farmhouse cooking,
it is this famous French casserole.

3½ cups dried great northern or other
white beans
2 pounds salt pork
4 large duck breasts
¼ cup olive oil
2 onions, chopped
6 garlic cloves, crushed
2 bay leaves
¼ teaspoon ground cloves
¼ cup tomato paste
8 good-quality sausages
4 tomatoes, skinned and quartered
1½ cups day-old white bread crumbs
salt and freshly ground black pepper

Serves 6–8

1

Put the beans in a large bowl and cover
with plenty of cold water. Let soak
overnight. If using salt pork,
soak it overnight in water, too.

2

Drain the beans and put them in a large
saucepan with fresh water to cover. Cover
and bring to a boil. Boil rapidly for
10 minutes. Drain and set the beans aside.

3

Drain the pork and cut it into large pieces,
discarding the rind. Halve the duck breasts.
Heat 2 tablespoons of the oil in a frying
pan and sauté the pork in batches until
it is browned.

NOTE
You can easily alter the proportions and
types of meat and vegetables in a cassoulet.
Turnips, carrots and celeriac make suitable
vegetable substitutes, while cubed lamb
and goose can replace the pork and duck.

4

Put the beans in a large, heavy saucepan
with the onions, garlic, bay leaves, ground
cloves and tomato paste. Stir in the
browned pork and just cover with water.
Bring to a boil, then reduce the heat to the
lowest setting and simmer, covered, for
about 1½ hours, until the beans are tender.

5

Preheat the oven to 350°F. Heat the
rest of the oil in a frying pan and sauté the
duck breasts and sausages until browned.
Cut the sausages into smaller pieces.
Transfer the bean mixture to a large
casserole. Stir in the sautéed sausages and
duck breasts and quartered tomatoes,
with salt and pepper to taste.

6

Sprinkle with an even layer of bread
crumbs. Bake for 45 minutes to 1 hour,
until the crust is golden. Serve hot.

Spicy Duck Breasts with Red Plums

Duck breasts can be bought separately, which makes this dish very easy to prepare.

INGREDIENTS

*4 duck breasts, 6 ounces
each, skinned
salt
2 teaspoons crushed stick cinnamon
4 tablespoons butter
1 tablespoon plum brandy (or Cognac)
1 cup chicken stock
1 cup heavy cream
pepper
6 fresh red plums, pitted and sliced
6 sprigs cilantro leaves, plus some
extra to garnish*

Serves 4

1

Preheat the oven to 375°F. Score the duck breasts and sprinkle with salt. Press the crushed cinnamon onto both sides of the duck breasts. Melt half the butter in a pan and fry them on both sides to seal, then place in an ovenproof dish with the butter and bake for 6–7 minutes.

2

Remove the dish from the oven and return the contents to the pan. Add the brandy and set it alight. When the flames have died down, remove from the pan and keep warm. Add the stock and cream to the pan and simmer gently until reduced and thick. Adjust the seasoning.

3

Reserve a few plum slices for garnishing. In a pan, melt the other half of the butter and fry the plums and cilantro, just enough to cook the fruit through. Slice the duck breasts and pour some sauce around each one, then garnish with slices of plum and chopped cilantro.

Duck Stew with Olives

*In this traditional method of preparing duck, the sweetness of the onions
balances the saltiness of the olives.*

INGREDIENTS

*2 ducks, about 3¼ pounds each,
quartered, or 8 duck leg quarters
1½ cups shallots, peeled
2 tablespoons all-purpose flour
1½ cups dry red wine
2 cups duck or chicken stock
1 bouquet garni
1 cup pitted green or black olives, or a
combination
salt, if needed, and freshly ground
black pepper*

Serves 6–8

3

Stir in the wine, then add the duck pieces,
stock and bouquet garni. Bring to a boil,
then reduce the heat, cover and simmer for
about 40 minutes, stirring occasionally.

4

Rinse the olives in several changes of cold
water. If they are very salty, put them in a
saucepan, cover with water and bring to a
boil, then drain and rinse. Add the pitted
olives to the casserole and continue
cooking for 20 minutes more, until the
duck is very tender.

5

Transfer the duck pieces, shallots and olives
to a plate. Strain the cooking liquid, skim
off all the fat and return the liquid to the
pan. Boil to reduce by about one-third,
then adjust the seasoning and return the
duck, shallots and olives to the casserole.
Simmer gently for a few minutes to heat
through and serve.

1

Put the duck portions, skin side down, in a
large frying pan. Cook over medium heat
for 10–12 minutes, until well browned,
then turn to color evenly. Cook in batches
if necessary.

2

Pour 1 tablespoon of the duck fat into a
large, flameproof casserole. Place the
casserole over medium heat and cook the
shallots until evenly browned, stirring
frequently. Sprinkle with the flour and cook
for 2 minutes more, stirring frequently.

Duck and Chestnut Casserole

*Serve this casserole with a mixture of mashed potatoes and celeriac,
to soak up the rich duck juices.*

INGREDIENTS

*4½ lb duck
3 tbsp olive oil
6 oz small onions
2 oz field mushrooms
2 oz shiitake mushrooms
1¼ cups dry red wine
such as Cabernet Sauvignon
1¼ cups beef stock,
fresh or canned
8 oz canned, peeled,
unsweetened chestnuts, drained
salt and freshly ground
black pepper*

Serves 4–6

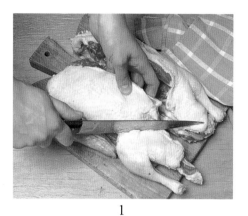

1

Cut the duck into eight pieces. Heat the oil
in a large frying pan and brown the duck
pieces. Remove from the frying pan.

2

Add the onions to the pan and brown them
well for 10 minutes.

3

Add the mushrooms and cook, stirring for
a few minutes more. Deglaze the pan with
the red wine and boil to reduce the
volume by half. Meanwhile, preheat the
oven to 350°F.

4

Pour the wine and the stock into a
casserole. Replace the duck, add the
chestnuts, season well and cook in the oven
for 1½ hours.

Roast Wild Duck with Mushroom Sauce

Wild duck is available in season from hunting friends and butchers specializing in game.
More strongly flavored than the domestic bird, wild duck combines well with dried morels.

INGREDIENTS

2 mallards (2½ pounds each) dressed
and barded weight
4 tablespoons (½ stick) butter
1 onion, halved and sliced
½ celery stalk, chopped
1 small carrot, chopped
5 tablespoons Madeira or sherry
10 large dried morel mushrooms
8 ounces wild mushrooms, trimmed and
sliced
2½ cups hot chicken stock
1 fresh thyme sprig
2 teaspoons wine vinegar
salt and freshly ground black pepper
parsley sprigs and carrot, cut into
short sticks, to garnish
roast potatoes, to serve

Serves 4

1

Preheat the oven to 375°F. Season the
ducks with salt and pepper. Heat half the
butter in a shallow pan and sauté the onion,
celery and carrot for 5 minutes. Using a
slotted spoon, transfer the vegetables to a
flameproof casserole that is large enough to
hold both ducks side by side.

2

Add the remaining butter to the shallow
pan. When it is hot, brown the ducks.
Place them in the casserole. Pour the
Madeira or sherry into the pan and bring to
a boil. Pour this liquid over the birds. Bake
for 40 minutes.

3

Tie the mushrooms in cheesecloth. Add the
stock and thyme to the casserole. Immerse
the cheesecloth bag in the liquid. Cover and
return to the oven for 40 minutes more.

4

Transfer the birds to a serving platter and keep
hot; set the mushrooms aside. Remove the
thyme from the braising liquid, then purée
the vegetables and liquid. Pour the purée back
into the casserole and stir the mushrooms into
the sauce. Add the vinegar and seasoning and
heat through gently. Garnish the ducks with
parsley and carrot. Serve with roast potatoes
and mushroom sauce.

Guinea Fowl with Cabbage

Guinea fowl is a domesticated relative of chicken, so chicken or pheasant can be used in this recipe.

INGREDIENTS

1 tablespoon vegetable oil
2½–3-pound guinea fowl, trussed
1 tablespoon butter
1 large onion, halved and sliced
1 large carrot, halved and sliced
1 large leek, sliced
1 pound green cabbage, such as Savoy, sliced or chopped
½ cup dry white wine
½ cup chicken stock
1 or 2 garlic cloves, finely chopped
salt and freshly ground black pepper

Serves 4

1

Preheat the oven to 350°F. Heat half the oil in a large, flameproof casserole and cook the guinea fowl until golden brown on all sides. Transfer to a plate.

2

Pour out the fat from the casserole and add the remaining oil with the butter. Cook the onion, carrot and leek over low heat for 5 minutes, stirring occasionally. Add the cabbage and cook, stirring occasionally, for 3–4 minutes, until slightly wilted. Season the vegetables with salt and pepper.

3

Place the guinea fowl on its side on the vegetables. Add the wine and bring to a boil, then add the stock and garlic. Cover and transfer to the oven. Cook for 25 minutes, then turn the bird onto the other side and cook for 20–25 minutes more, until it is tender and the juices run clear when the thickest part of the thigh is pierced with a knife.

4

Transfer the bird to a board and let stand for 5–10 minutes, then cut into four or eight pieces. With a slotted spoon, transfer the cabbage to a warmed serving dish and place the guinea fowl on top. Skim any fat from the cooking juices and serve the juices separately.

Roast Pheasant with Port

Many farmers—and their fortunate friends—have a regular supply of pheasant in the hunting season. This is an excellent way of cooking them.

INGREDIENTS

2 oven-ready pheasants, about
1½ pounds each
4 tablespoons (½ stick) butter, softened
8 fresh thyme sprigs
2 bay leaves
6 lean bacon strips
1 tablespoon all-purpose flour
¾ cup game or chicken stock, plus more
if needed
1 tablespoon red currant jelly
3–4 tablespoons port
freshly ground black pepper

Serves 4

1

Preheat the oven to 450°F. Line a large roasting pan with a sheet of heavy-duty foil large enough to enclose the pheasants. Lightly brush the foil with oil.

2

Wipe the pheasants with damp paper towels and remove any extra fat or skin. Using your fingertips, carefully loosen the skin of the breasts. Spread the butter between the skin and breast meat of each bird. Tie the legs securely with string, then lay the thyme sprigs and a bay leaf over the breast of each bird.

3

Lay the bacon over the breasts, place the birds in the foil-lined pan and season with pepper. Bring up the foil and enclose the birds. Roast for 20 minutes, then reduce the oven temperature to 375°F and cook for 40 minutes more.

4

Uncover the birds and roast 10–15 minutes more. Transfer the birds to a board and let stand for 10 minutes before carving.

5

Pour the juices into the roasting pan and skim off any fat. Sprinkle in the flour and stir over a medium heat until smooth. Whisk in the stock and red currant jelly and bring to a boil. Simmer until the sauce thickens slightly, then stir in the port and adjust the seasoning. Strain and serve with the pheasants.

Braised Pheasant with Cèpes, Chestnuts and Bacon

Toward the end of their season pheasant can be a little tough, so they are best braised. Try this delicious casserole enriched with wild mushrooms and chestnuts.

INGREDIENTS

2 mature pheasants
4 tablespoons (½ stick) butter
5 tablespoons brandy
12 button or pickling onions, peeled
1 celery stalk, chopped
2 ounces unsmoked lean bacon, cut into strips
3 tablespoons all-purpose flour
2¼ cups hot chicken stock
1½ cups peeled chestnuts
3 cups fresh cèpes or other wild mushrooms, trimmed and sliced, or ¼ cup dried cèpes, soaked in warm water for 20 minutes
1 tablespoon lemon juice
salt and freshly ground black pepper
watercress sprigs, to garnish

Serves 4

2

Melt the remaining butter. Lightly brown the onions, celery and bacon. Stir in the flour, cook for 1 minute, then gradually stir in the hot stock. Add the chestnuts and mushrooms, then the pheasants and their juices. Bring to a gentle simmer, cover and cook in the oven for 1½ hours, or until thoroughly cooked.

3

Transfer the pheasants and vegetables to a serving plate. Skim off any fat from the gravy, bring it back to a boil, add the lemon juice and season to taste. Pour the gravy into a gravy boat and garnish the birds with watercress sprigs.

1

Preheat the oven to 325°F. Season the pheasants with salt and pepper. Melt half the butter in a large, flameproof casserole and brown the birds all over. Transfer to a shallow dish. Pour off the cooking fat and return the casserole to the heat. Stir the sediment until it has browned. Stand back and add the brandy (the sudden flames will die down quickly). Stir to incorporate the sediment, then pour the juices over the pheasant.

Squab Pie

This recipe, for a phyllo pie filled with an unusual but delicious mixture of squab, eggs, spices and nuts, is based upon a traditional dish. Chicken can be used instead of squab.

INGREDIENTS

3 squabs
4 tablespoons (½ stick) butter
1 onion, chopped
1 cinnamon stick
½ teaspoon ground ginger
2 tablespoons chopped fresh cilantro
3 tablespoons chopped fresh parsley
pinch of ground turmeric
1 tablespoon sugar
¼ teaspoon ground cinnamon
1 cup toasted almonds, finely chopped
6 eggs, beaten
salt and freshly ground black pepper
cinnamon and confectioners' sugar, to garnish

For the pastry
¾ cup butter, melted
16 sheets phyllo pastry
1 egg yolk

Serves 6

1

Wash the squabs and place them in a heavy pan with the butter, onion, cinnamon stick, ginger, cilantro, parsley and turmeric. Season with salt and pepper. Add just enough water to cover and bring to a boil. Reduce the heat, cover and simmer gently for about 1 hour, until the squab flesh is very tender.

2

Strain off the stock and reserve. Skin and bone the squabs, and shred the flesh into bite-size pieces. Preheat the oven to 350°F. Mix the sugar, cinnamon and almonds in a bowl.

3

Measure ⅔ cup of the reserved stock into a small pan. Add the eggs and mix well. Stir over low heat until creamy and very thick and almost set. Season with salt and pepper.

4

Brush a 12-inch diameter ovenproof dish with some of the melted butter and lay the first sheet of pastry in the dish. Brush this with butter and continue with five more sheets of pastry. Cover with the almond mixture, then half the egg mixture. Moisten with a little stock.

5

Layer four more sheets of filo pastry, brushing with butter as before. Lay the squab meat on top, then add the remaining egg mixture and more stock. Cover with all the remaining pastry, brushing each sheet with butter, and tuck in any overlap.

6

Brush the pie with egg yolk and bake for 40 minutes. Raise the oven temperature to 400°F and bake for 15 minutes more, until the pastry is crisp and golden. Garnish with cinnamon and confectioners' sugar in a lattice design. Serve hot.

Rabbit Sauté

Rabbit has always been a farmhouse favorite. City folk eager to try this recipe should look for packages of rabbit pieces, sold at the supermarket.

INGREDIENTS

1½ pounds rabbit pieces
1¼ cups dry white wine
1 tablespoon sherry vinegar
several fresh oregano sprigs
2 bay leaves
1 fresh red chili
6 tablespoons olive oil
6 ounces pearl onions or shallots, peeled
4 garlic cloves, sliced
2 teaspoons paprika
⅔ cup chicken stock
salt and freshly ground black pepper
Italian parsley sprigs, to garnish

Serves 4

1

Put the rabbit in a bowl. Add the wine, vinegar, oregano and bay leaves and toss lightly. Cover and marinate for several hours or overnight.

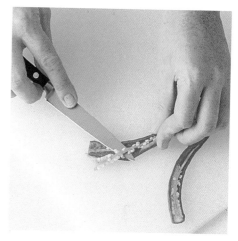

2

Remove the seeds from the chili and chop it finely. Set it aside. Drain the rabbit pieces, reserving the marinade, and pat dry on paper towels. Heat the oil in a large frying pan and fry the rabbit on all sides until golden, then remove with a slotted spoon. Fry the onions until beginning to color.

NOTE
If more convenient, bake the stew in an ovenproof dish at 350°F for about 50 minutes.

3

Remove the onions from the pan and add the chili, garlic and paprika. Cook, stirring, for about 1 minute. Add the reserved marinade, with the stock. Season lightly.

4

Return the rabbit to the pan with the onions. Bring to a boil, then reduce the heat, cover and simmer for about 45 minutes, until the rabbit is tender. Serve, garnished with a few sprigs of flat-leaf parsley, if desired.

Casseroled Rabbit with Thyme

This is the sort of home cooking found in farmhouse kitchens and cozy neighborhood restaurants in France, where rabbit is treated much like chicken and enjoyed frequently.

INGREDIENTS

6 tablespoons all-purpose flour
2½-pound rabbit, cut into 8 pieces
1 tablespoon butter
1 tablespoon olive oil
1 cup red wine
1½–2 cups chicken stock
1 tablespoon fresh thyme leaves
1 bay leaf
2 garlic cloves, finely chopped
2–3 teaspoons Dijon mustard
salt and freshly ground black pepper

Serves 4

1

Put the flour in a strong plastic bag and season with salt and pepper. One at a time, drop the rabbit pieces into the bag and shake to coat them with flour. Tap off the excess, then discard any remaining flour.

2

Melt the butter and oil in a flameproof casserole. Cook the rabbit pieces until golden.

3

Pour in the wine and boil for 1 minute, then add enough of the stock just to cover the meat. Add the herbs and garlic. Cover and simmer gently for 1 hour.

4

Stir in the mustard. Lift the rabbit pieces onto a serving platter. Season the sauce, then strain it over the rabbit.

Farmhouse Venison Pie

This satisfying pie combines venison in a rich gravy with a potato and parsnip topping.

INGREDIENTS

3 tablespoons sunflower oil
1 onion, chopped
1 garlic clove, crushed
3 lean bacon strips, chopped
1½ pounds ground venison
1 cup button mushrooms, chopped
2 tablespoons all-purpose flour
2 cups beef stock
⅔ cup ruby port
2 bay leaves
1 teaspoon chopped fresh thyme
1 teaspoon Dijon mustard
1 tablespoon red currant jelly
1½ pounds potatoes, peeled and cut
into large chunks
1 pounds parsnips, peeled and cut into
large chunks
1 egg yolk
4 tablespoons (½ stick) butter
grated nutmeg
3 tablespoons chopped fresh parsley
salt and freshly ground black pepper

Serves 4

2

Meanwhile, preheat the oven to 400°F .
Bring a saucepan of lightly salted water to
a boil and cook the potatoes and parsnips
for 20 minutes, or until tender. Drain and
mash, then beat in the egg yolk, butter,
nutmeg and chopped parsley. Season to
taste with salt and pepper.

3

Spoon the venison mixture into a large pie
dish. Level the surface. Spread the potato
and parsnip mixture over the meat and
bake for 30–40 minutes, until piping hot
and golden brown. Serve immediately.

1

Heat the oil in a large frying pan and fry
the onion, garlic and bacon for 5 minutes.
Add the venison and mushrooms and cook
for a few minutes, stirring, until browned.
Stir in the flour and cook for 1–2 minutes,
then add the stock, port, herbs, mustard,
red currant jelly and seasoning. Bring to a
boil, cover and simmer for 30–40 minutes,
until tender.

Meat Dishes

In farmhouses all over the world, main meals mean meat. Robust roasts, meat loaves and pot pies are very popular, but it is the stew that reigns supreme. Simmered for hours in rich stock flavored with wine, herbs and aromatic vegetables, meat becomes meltingly tender. The following section is packed with hearty meat recipes to choose from to suit the time available and the occasion in mind.

Lamb Stew with Vegetables

*This farmhouse stew is made with lamb and a selection of young tender spring vegetables,
such as carrots, new potatoes, pearl onions, peas, green beans and turnips.*

INGREDIENTS

¼ cup vegetable oil
3–3½ pounds lamb shoulder, trimmed
and cut into 2-inch pieces
½ cup water
3–4 tablespoons all-purpose flour
4 cups lamb stock
1 large bouquet garni
3 garlic cloves, lightly crushed
3 ripe tomatoes, skinned, seeded and
chopped
1 teaspoon tomato paste
1½ pounds small potatoes, peeled or
scrubbed
12 baby carrots, scrubbed

4 ounces green beans, cut into
2-inch pieces
2 tablespoons butter
12–18 pearl onions or shallots, peeled
6 medium turnips, quartered
2 tablespoons sugar
¼ teaspoon dried thyme
1¼ cups peas
½ cup snow peas
salt and freshly ground pepper
3 tablespoons chopped fresh parsley or
cilantro, to garnish

Serves 6

1

Heat half the oil in a large, heavy frying
pan. Brown the lamb in batches, adding
more oil if needed, and transfer it to
a large, flameproof casserole. Add
3 tablespoons of the water to the pan and
boil for about 1 minute, stirring and
scraping the base of the pan, then pour the
liquid into the casserole.

4

About 1½ hours before serving, take the
casserole from the refrigerator, lift off the
solid fat and blot the surface with paper
towels to remove all traces of fat. Set the
casserole over medium heat and bring to a
simmer. Cook the potatoes in a pan of
boiling, salted water for 15–20 minutes,
then transfer to a bowl and add the carrots
to the same water. Cook for 4–5 minutes
and transfer to the same bowl. Add the
green beans and boil for 2–3 minutes.
Transfer to the bowl with the other
vegetables.

2

Sprinkle the flour over the browned meat
in the casserole and set it over medium
heat. Cook for 3–5 minutes, until browned.
Stir in the stock, the bouquet garni, garlic,
tomatoes and tomato paste. Season with salt
and pepper.

3

Bring to a boil over high heat. Skim the
surface, reduce the heat and simmer,
stirring occasionally, for about 1 hour, until
the meat is tender. Cool the stew to room
temperature, cover and chill overnight.

5

(Left) Melt the butter in a heavy frying pan
and add the onions and turnips with
another 3 tablespoons water. Cover and
cook for 4–5 minutes. Stir in the sugar and
thyme and cook until the vegetables are
shiny and caramelized. Transfer them to the
bowl of vegetables. Add the remaining
2 tablespoons water to the pan. Boil for
1 minute, incorporating the sediment, then
add this liquid to the lamb.

6

When the lamb and gravy are hot, add the
cooked vegetables to the stew and stir
gently to distribute. Stir in the peas and
snow peas and cook for 5 minutes, until
they turn a bright green, then stir in
2 tablespoons of the parsley or cilantro.
Pour the stew into a large, warmed serving
dish. Scatter the remaining parsley or
cilantro on top and serve.

Roast Leg of Lamb with Wild Mushroom Stuffing

*Removing the thigh bone creates a cavity that can be filled with
a wild mushroom stuffing—the perfect treat for Sunday lunch.*

INGREDIENTS

*4–4½-pound leg of lamb, boned
salt and freshly ground black pepper
watercress, to garnish*

For the wild mushroom stuffing
*2 tablespoons butter, plus extra for
gravy
1 shallot or small onion, minced
8 ounces assorted wild and
cultivated mushrooms*

*½ garlic clove, crushed
1 fresh thyme sprig, chopped
1 ounce crustless white bread, diced
2 egg yolks*

For the wild mushroom gravy
*¼ cup red wine
1⅔ cups hot chicken stock
2 tablespoons dried cèpes, soaked in
boiling water for 20 minutes*

*4 teaspoons cornstarch
1 teaspoon Dijon mustard
1 tablespoon water
½ teaspoon wine vinegar
pat of butter*

Serves 4

1

Preheat the oven to 400°F. To make
the stuffing, melt the butter in a large,
nonstick frying pan and gently fry the
shallot or onion without coloring. Add
the mushrooms, garlic and thyme. Stir
until the mushroom juices begin to run,
then increase the heat so that they
evaporate completely.

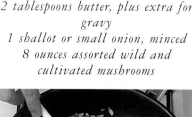

4

Place the lamb in a roasting pan. Roast
for 15 minutes per 1 pound for rare meat
and 20 minutes per 1 pound for medium-
rare. A 4-pound leg will take 1 hour and
20 minutes if cooked medium-rare.

2

Transfer the mushrooms to a mixing bowl
and add the bread and egg yolks. Season
with salt and pepper and mix well. Allow
to cool slightly.

5

Transfer the lamb to a warmed serving
plate. To make the gravy, spoon off all
excess fat from the roasting pan and brown
the sediment over medium heat. Add the
wine and stir in the chicken stock and the
mushrooms, with their soaking liquid.

3

Season the inside of the lamb cavity, then
spoon in the stuffing. Tie up the end with
string and then tie around the joint so that
it does not lose its shape.

6

Mix the cornstarch and mustard in a cup;
blend in the water. Stir into the stock
mixture to thicken it. Add the vinegar.
Season and stir in the butter. Garnish the
lamb with watercress and serve with the
wild mushroom gravy.

Lamb with Mint and Lemon

Lamb has been served with mint for many years – it is a great combination.

8 lamb steaks, 8 ounces each
grated rind and juice of 1 lemon
2 cloves garlic, peeled and crushed
2 scallions, finely chopped
2 teaspoons finely chopped fresh mint
leaves, plus some leaves for
garnishing
4 tablespoons extra virgin olive oil
salt and black pepper

Serves 8

1

Make a marinade for the lamb by mixing all the other ingredients and seasoning to taste. Place the lamb steaks in a shallow dish and cover with the marinade. Refrigerate overnight.

2

Broil the lamb under high heat until just cooked, basting with the marinade occasionally during cooking. Turn once during cooking. Serve garnished with fresh mint leaves.

Lamb Pie with Pear, Ginger and Mint Sauce

Cooking lamb with fruit is an idea taken from traditional Persian cuisine.

1 boned mid-loin of lamb, 2 pounds
after boning
salt and pepper
8 large sheets filo pastry
scant 2 tablespoons butter

For the stuffing
1 tablespoon butter
1 small onion, chopped
1 cup whole-wheat bread crumbs
grated rind of 1 lemon
6 ounces drained canned pears from a

14-ounce can (rest
of can, and juice, used for sauce)
¼ teaspoon ground ginger
salt and pepper
1 small egg, beaten
skewers, string and large needle to
make roll

For the sauce
rest of can of pears, including juice
2 teaspoons finely chopped fresh mint

Serves 6

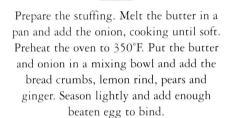

1

Prepare the stuffing. Melt the butter in a pan and add the onion, cooking until soft. Preheat the oven to 350°F. Put the butter and onion in a mixing bowl and add the bread crumbs, lemon rind, pears and ginger. Season lightly and add enough beaten egg to bind.

2

Spread the loin out flat, fat side down, and season. Place the stuffing along the middle of the loin and roll carefully, holding it with skewers while you sew it together with string. Place in a large baking pan and brown the loin slowly on all sides. This will take 20–30 minutes. Let cool, and store in the refrigerator until needed.

3

Preheat the oven to 400°F. Take two sheets of filo pastry and brush with melted butter. Overlap by about 5 inches to make a square. Place the next two sheets on top and brush with butter. Continue until all the pastry has been used.

4

Place the roll of lamb diagonally across one corner of the pastry, without overlapping the sides. Fold the corner over the lamb, fold in the sides, and brush the pastry well with melted butter. Roll to the far corner of the sheet. Place, seam side down, on a buttered baking sheet and brush all over with the rest of the melted butter. Bake for about 30 minutes or until golden brown.

5

Blend the remaining pears with their juice and the mint, and serve with the lamb.

Lamb and Leeks with Mint and Scallions

*If you do not have any homemade chicken stock, use a good
quality ready-made stock rather than a bouillon cube.*

INGREDIENTS

2 tablespoons sunflower oil
4 pounds lamb
10 scallions, thickly sliced
3 leeks, thickly sliced
1 tablespoon flour
²⁄₃ cup white wine
1¹⁄₃ cup chicken stock
1 tablespoon tomato paste
1 tablespoon sugar
salt and pepper
2 tablespoons fresh mint leaves, finely
chopped, plus a few more to garnish
4 ounces dried pears, chopped
2 pounds potatoes, peeled and sliced
2 tablespoons melted butter

Serves 6

1

Heat the oil and fry the cubed lamb
to seal it. Transfer to a casserole. Preheat
the oven to 350°F.

2

Fry the scallions and leeks for 1 minute,
stir in the flour and cook for another
minute. Add the wine and stock and bring
to a boil. Add the tomato paste, sugar, salt
and pepper with the mint and chopped
pears and pour into the casserole. Stir the
mixture. Arrange the sliced potatoes on top
and brush with the melted butter.

3

Cover and bake for 1½ hours. Then
increase the temperature to 400°F,
and cook for 30 more minutes,
uncovered, to brown the potatoes.
Garnish with mint leaves.

Pork Sausage and Puff Pastry Strudel

Country butchers sell a wonderful variety of sausages, including venison, pork and apple, and herb. All taste delicious when wrapped around a wild mushroom filling and baked in pastry.

INGREDIENTS

4 tablespoons (½ stick) butter
½ garlic clove, crushed
1 tablespoon chopped fresh thyme
1 pound assorted wild and cultivated mushrooms, sliced
1 cup fresh white bread crumbs
5 tablespoons chopped fresh parsley
12 ounces puff pastry
1½ pounds best-quality pork sausages
1 egg, beaten with a pinch of salt
salt and freshly ground black pepper

Serves 4

3

Make a series of slanting 1-inch cuts in the pastry on either side of the filling. Fold each end of the pastry over the filling, moisten the pastry with beaten egg and then cross the top with alternate strips of pastry from each side. Allow the pastry to rest for 40 minutes. Preheat the oven to 350°F. Brush the pastry with a little more egg and bake for 1 hour.

1

Melt the butter in a large frying pan and soften the garlic, thyme and mushrooms gently for 5–6 minutes. When the mushroom juices begin to run, increase the heat to boil off the liquid, then stir in the bread crumbs, parsley and seasoning.

2

Roll out the pastry on a floured surface to a 14 x 10-inch rectangle. Place on a large baking sheet. Skin the sausages. Place half of the sausage meat in a 5-inch strip along the center of the pastry. Cover with the mushroom mixture, then with the rest of the sausage.

Pork and Black Bean Stew

This simple Spanish stew uses a few robust ingredients to create a deliciously intense flavor.

INGREDIENTS

*1½ cups dried black beans, soaked
overnight
1½ pounds bacon
¼ cup olive oil
12 ounces pearl onions or shallots
2 celery stalks, thickly sliced
2 teaspoons paprika
5 ounces chorizo sausage, chopped
2½ cups chicken or vegetable stock
2 green bell peppers, seeded and cut
into large pieces
salt and freshly ground pepper*

Serves 5–6

1

Preheat the oven to 325°F. Drain the beans, place them in a saucepan and cover with fresh water. Bring to a boil, boil rapidly for 10 minutes, then drain. Cut off any rind from the bacon and cut it into large chunks.

2

Heat the oil in a large frying pan and fry the onions or shallots and celery for 3 minutes. Add the bacon and fry for 5–10 minutes, until the bacon is browned. Stir in the paprika and chorizo and fry for 2 minutes more. Transfer to an ovenproof dish, add the beans and mix well.

3

Add the stock to the pan and bring to a boil. Season lightly, then pour over the meat and beans. Cover and bake for 1 hour, then stir in the green bell peppers. Bake for 15 minutes more, and serve hot.

NOTE

This is a good-natured stew that works well with any winter vegetable. Try adding chunks of leek, turnip, celeriac and even small potatoes.

Pork and Sausage Casserole

This dish is based on a rural Spanish recipe. You may be able to find the butifarra sausages in a Spanish market but, if not, sweet Italian sausages will do.

INGREDIENTS

2 tablespoons olive oil
4 boneless pork chops, about 6 ounces
4 butifarra or sweet Italian sausages
1 onion, chopped
2 garlic cloves, chopped
½ cup dry white wine
4 plum tomatoes, chopped
1 bay leaf
2 tablespoons chopped fresh parsley
salt and freshly ground black pepper
green salad and baked potatoes, to serve

Serves 4

NOTE
Vine tomatoes, which are making a
welcome appearance in supermarkets, can
be used instead of plum tomatoes.

1

Heat the oil in a large, deep frying pan.
Cook the pork chops over high heat until
browned on both sides, then transfer
to a plate.

2

Add the sausages, onion and garlic to the
pan and cook over moderate heat until the
sausages are browned and the onion
softened, turning the sausages two or three
times during cooking. Return the chops
to the pan.

3

Stir in the wine, tomatoes and bay leaf, and
season with salt and pepper. Add the
parsley. Cover the pan and cook for
30 minutes.

4

Remove the sausages from the pan and cut
into thick slices. Return them to the pan
and heat through. Serve hot, accompanied
by a green salad and baked potatoes.

Country Pie

A classic raised pie. It takes quite a long time to make,
but is a perfect winter treat.

1

Cut as much meat from the raw duck and chicken as possible, removing the skin and sinews. Cut the duck and chicken breasts into cubes and set them aside.

2

Mix the rest of the duck and chicken meat with the minced pork, egg, shallots, spices, Worcestershire sauce, lemon rind and salt and pepper. Add the red wine and leave for about 15 minutes for the flavors to develop.

3

To make the aspic, place the meat bones and trimmings, carrots, onion, celery, wine, bay leaf and clove in a large pan and cover with 12½ cups of water. Bring to a boil, skimming off any scum, and simmer gently for 2½ hours.

4

To make the pastry, place the fat and water in a pan and bring to a boil. Sift the flour with a pinch of salt into a bowl and pour on the hot liquid. Mix with a wooden spoon, and, when the dough is cool enough to handle, knead it well and let it sit in a warm place, covered with a cloth, for 20–30 minutes or until you are ready to use it. Preheat the oven to 400°F.

5

Grease a 10 in loose-based deep cake pan. Roll out about two-thirds of the pastry thinly enough to line the cake pan. Make sure there are no holes and allow enough pastry to leave a little hanging over the top. Fill the pie with a layer of half the minced-pork mixture; then top this with a layer of the cubed duck and chicken breast-meat and cubes of ham. Top with the remaining minced pork. Brush the overhanging edges of pastry with water and cover with the remaining rolled-out pastry. Seal the edges well. Make two large holes in the top and decorate with any pastry trimmings.

6

Bake the pie for 30 minutes. Brush the top with the egg and salt mixture. Turn down the oven to 350°F. After 30 minutes loosely cover the pie with foil to prevent the top getting too brown, and bake it for a further 1 hour.

7

Strain the stock after 2½ hours. Let it cool and remove the solidified layer of fat from the surface. Measure 2½ cups of stock. Heat it gently to just below boiling point and whisk the gelatin into it until no lumps are left. Add the remaining strained stock and leave to cool.

8

When the pie is cool, place a funnel through one of the holes and pour in as much of the stock as possible, letting it come up to the holes in the crust. Leave to set for at least 24 hours before slicing and serving.

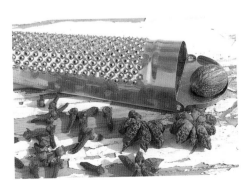

Slow-cooked Beef Stew

In its native Provence, this is called a daube, and takes the name from the daubière, the earthenware pot it was traditionally cooked in. It is improved by being cooked a day ahead.

INGREDIENTS

2–4 tablespoons olive oil
8 ounces lean salt pork or thick-cut lean bacon, diced
4–4½ pounds stewing beef, cut into 3-inch pieces
3 cups red wine
4 carrots, thickly sliced
2 large onions, coarsely chopped
3 tomatoes, skinned, seeded and chopped
1 tablespoon tomato paste
2–4 garlic cloves, very finely chopped
1 bouquet garni
1 teaspoon black peppercorns
1 small onion, studded with 4 cloves
grated zest and juice of 1 orange
2–3 tablespoons chopped parsley
salt and freshly ground black pepper

Serves 6–8

1

Heat 2 tablespoons of the olive oil in a large, heavy frying pan and cook the salt pork or bacon, stirring frequently, until the fat runs. Raise the heat and cook for 4–5 minutes more, until browned. Transfer with a slotted spoon to a large, flameproof casserole.

2

Add enough beef to the frying pan to fit easily in one layer. Cook for 6–8 minutes, until browned, turning to color all sides, then transfer the meat to the casserole. Brown the rest of the meat in the same way, adding a little more oil if needed.

3

Pour in the wine and, if needed, add water to cover the beef and bacon. Bring to a boil over medium heat, skimming off any foam that rises to the surface.

4

Stir in the carrots, onions, tomatoes, tomato paste, garlic, bouquet garni, peppercorns and clove-studded onion. Cover tightly and simmer over low heat for about 3 hours. Skim off any fat. Season, discard the bouquet garni and clove-studded onion and stir in the orange zest and juice and the parsley.

Beef Casserole with Beans

This hearty casserole is slow-cooked to ensure that the meat is beautifully tender.

INGREDIENTS

*1¼ cups dried navy or lima beans,
soaked overnight in water
2–4 tablespoons oil
10 small onions, halved
2 carrots, diced
3–3½ pounds beef stew, cubed
6 small hard-cooked eggs in their
shells
1 teaspoon paprika
1 teaspoon tomato paste
2½ cups boiling water or beef stock
salt and freshly ground black pepper*

Serves 6–8

NOTE

If you have one, use a large slow cooker to cook the stew. You should not need to add extra liquid.

1

Preheat the oven to 225°F. Drain the beans, place them in a saucepan and cover with fresh water. Bring to a boil. Cook rapidly for 10 minutes, skimming off the white froth and any bean skins that come to the surface. Drain.

2

Heat half the oil in a frying pan and sauté the onions for about 10 minutes, then transfer to a casserole with the carrots and beans. Heat the remaining oil and brown the beef in batches. Place it on top of the vegetables. Tuck the eggs between the pieces of meat.

3

Stir the paprika and tomato paste into the oil left in the pan. Add a generous sprinkling of salt and pepper and cook for 1 minute. Stir in the boiling water or stock to incorporate the sediment, then pour the mixture over the meat and eggs.

4

Cover the casserole and cook for at least 8 hours, or until the meat is very tender, adding more liquid as needed. Take out the eggs, remove the shells and return the eggs to the casserole before serving.

Beef Rib with Onion Sauce

Beef with a peppercorn crust, seared in a pan and then briefly roasted in the oven, feeds two hungry farm workers or four people with less hearty appetites. The onion sauce is superb.

INGREDIENTS

1 beef rib with bone, about
2¼ pounds and about 1½ inches thick,
well trimmed of fat
1 teaspoon lightly crushed black
peppercorns
1 tablespoon coarse sea salt, crushed
4 tablespoons (½ stick) butter
1 large red onion, sliced
½ cup fruity red wine
½ cup beef stock
1–2 tablespoons red currant jelly
¼ teaspoon dried thyme
2–3 tablespoons olive oil
salt and freshly ground black pepper

Serves 2–4

1

Wipe the beef with damp paper towels. Mix the crushed peppercorns with the crushed salt and press the mixture onto both sides of the meat, coating it completely. Let stand, loosely covered, for 30 minutes.

2

Meanwhile, make the onion sauce. Melt 3 tablespoons of the butter in a saucepan and cook the onion for 3–5 minutes, until softened. Add the wine, stock, red currant jelly and thyme and bring to a boil. Reduce the heat and simmer for 30–35 minutes, until the liquid has evaporated and the sauce has thickened. Season with salt and pepper and keep hot.

3

Preheat the oven to 425°F. Melt the remaining butter with the oil in a heavy, ovenproof frying pan. Add the meat and sear over high heat for 1–2 minutes on each side. Immediately place the pan in the oven and roast for 8–10 minutes. Transfer the beef to a board, cover loosely and let stand for 10 minutes. With a knife, loosen the meat from the rib bone, then carve into thick slices. Serve with the onion sauce.

Country Meat Loaf

This dish makes a delicious alternative to a roast.

INGREDIENTS

2 tablespoons butter
1 small onion, finely chopped
2 garlic cloves, crushed
2 celery stalks, finely chopped
2 cups ground lean beef
2 cups ground pork
2 eggs
1 cup fresh white bread crumbs
3 tablespoons chopped fresh parsley
2 tablespoons snipped fresh basil
½ teaspoon fresh thyme leaves
½ teaspoon salt
½ teaspoon freshly ground black pepper
2 tablespoons Worcestershire sauce
¼ cup chili sauce or ketchup
6 lean bacon strips
fresh basil sprigs, to garnish

Serve 6

3

Use your hands to shape the meat mixture into an oval loaf. Carefully transfer it to a roasting pan.

4

Lay the bacon slices across the meat loaf. Bake for 1¼ hours, basting occasionally. Remove from the oven and drain off the fat. Place the meat loaf on a platter and let stand for 10 minutes before serving, garnished with basil.

1

Preheat the oven to 350°F. Melt the butter in a small frying pan. Cook the onion, garlic and celery over low heat for 8–10 minutes, until softened. Remove from the heat and let cool slightly.

2

In a large mixing bowl combine the onion, garlic and celery with all the other ingredients except the bacon and basil. Mix together lightly.

155

Sunday Best Beef Wellington

*For a special occasion, nothing surpasses the succulent flavor of Beef Wellington.
Traditionally, the beef is spread with goose liver pâté, but many country cooks prefer a pâté
made from woodland mushrooms; use a variety with maximum flavor.*

INGREDIENTS

*1½ pounds fillet of beef, tied
1 tablespoons vegetable oil
12 ounces puff pastry
1 egg, beaten, to glaze
salt and freshly ground black pepper*

*For the parsley pancakes
½ cup all-purpose flour
⅔ cup milk
1 egg
2 tablespoons chopped fresh parsley*

*For the mushroom pâté
2 tablespoons butter
2 shallots or 1 small onion, chopped
4 cups assorted wild and cultivated
mushrooms, chopped
1 cup fresh white bread crumbs
5 tablespoons heavy cream
2 egg yolks*

Serves 4

1

Preheat the oven to 425°F. Season the fillet
with several grindings of black pepper.
Heat the oil in a roasting pan, add the beef
and quickly sear to brown all sides. Transfer
to the oven and roast for
15 minutes for rare, 20 minutes for
medium-rare or 25 minutes for well-done
meat. Set aside to cool. Reduce the oven
temperature to 375°F.

2

To make the pancakes, beat the flour, a
pinch of salt, half the milk, the egg and
parsley together until smooth, then stir in
the remaining milk. Heat a greased,
nonstick pan and pour in enough batter to
coat the bottom. When set, turn the
pancake over and cook the other side briefly
until lightly browned. Continue with the
remaining batter—the recipe makes
three or four pancakes.

3

To make the mushroom pâté, melt the
butter in a frying pan and fry the shallots
or onion for 7–10 minutes to soften
without coloring. Add the mushrooms and
cook until the juices run. Increase the heat
so that the juices evaporate. Combine the
bread crumbs, cream and egg yolks. Add
the mushroom mixture and mix to a
smooth paste. Let cool.

4

Roll out the pastry to a 14 x 12-inch
rectangle. Place two pancakes on the pastry
and spread with mushroom pâté. Place the
beef on top and spread with any remaining
pâté, then add the remaining pancakes. Cut
out and reserve four squares from the corners
of the pastry, then moisten the pastry with
egg and wrap the meat. Decorate with the
reserved pastry trimmings.

5

Put the Beef Wellington on a baking sheet
and brush evenly with beaten egg. Bake for
about 40 minutes, until golden brown. To
ensure that the meat is heated through, test
with a meat thermometer. It should read
125–130°F for rare, 135°F for medium-rare
and 160°F for well-done meat.

Roast Beef with Porcini and Sweet Bell Peppers

A substantial and warming dish for cold, dark evenings.

INGREDIENTS

3–3½ lb piece of sirloin
1 tbsp olive oil
1 lb small red bell peppers
4 oz mushrooms
6 oz thick-sliced pancetta
or bacon, cubed
2 tbsp all-purpose flour
⅔ cup full-bodied
red wine
1¼ cups beef stock
2 tbsp Marsala
2 tsp dried mixed herbs
salt and freshly ground
black pepper

Serves 8

_1_

Preheat the oven to 375°F. Season the meat
well. Heat the olive oil in a large frying pan.
When very hot, brown the meat on all sides.
Place in a large roasting pan and cook
for 1¼ hours.

_2_

Put the red peppers in the oven to roast for
20 minutes, if small ones are available, or
45 minutes if large ones are used.

_3_

Near the end of the meat's cooking time,
prepare the gravy. Coarsely chop the
mushroom caps and stems.

_4_

Heat the frying pan again and add the
pancetta or bacon. Cook until the fat runs
freely from the meat. Add the flour and cook
for a few minutes until browned.

_5_

Gradually stir in the red wine and the stock.
Bring to a boil, stirring. Lower the heat
and add the Marsala, herbs and seasoning.

_6_

Add the mushrooms to the pan and heat
through. Remove the sirloin from the oven
and leave to stand for 10 minutes before
carving it. Serve with the roasted peppers
and the hot gravy.

Traditional Beef Stew and Dumplings

This dish can cook in the oven while you go for a wintery walk to work up an appetite.

INGREDIENTS

1 tbsp all-purpose flour
2½ lb stewing beef,
cubed
2 tbsp olive oil
2 large onions, sliced
1 lb carrots, sliced
½ pint / 1¼ cups Guinness
or dark beer
3 bay leaves
2 tsp brown sugar
3 fresh thyme sprigs
1 tsp cider vinegar
salt and freshly ground
black pepper

For the dumplings
½ cup chopped Crisco
2 cups self-rising
flour
2 tbsp chopped mixed
fresh herbs
about ⅔ cup water

Serves 6

1

Preheat the oven to 325°F. Season the flour
and sprinkle over the meat, tossing to coat.

2

Heat the oil in a large casserole and lightly
sauté the onions and carrots. Remove the
vegetables with a slotted spoon and
reserve them.

3

Brown the meat well in batches
in the casserole.

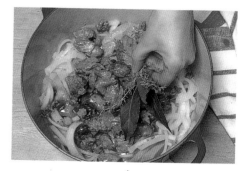

4

Return all the vegetables to the casserole and
add any leftover seasoned flour. Add the
Guinness or beer, bay leaves, sugar and
thyme. Bring the liquid to a boil and then
transfer to the oven.

6

Form the dough into small balls with floured
hands. Add the cider vinegar to the meat and
spoon the dumplings on top. Cook for a
further 20 minutes, until the dumplings
have cooked through and serve hot.

5

After the meat has been cooking for 1 hour
and 40 minutes, make the dumplings. Mix
the Crisco and flour together. Add enough
water to make a soft, sticky dough.

Steak and Kidney Pie, with Mustard and Bay Gravy

This is a sharpened-up, bay-flavored version of a traditional favorite. The fragrant mustard, bay and parsley perfectly complement the flavor of the beef.

INGREDIENTS

1 pound puff pastry
2½ tablespoons flour
salt and pepper
1½ pounds rump steak, cubed
6 ounces pig's or lamb's kidney
scant 2 tablespoons butter
1 medium onion, chopped
1 tablespoon English mustard
2 bay leaves
1 tablespoon chopped parsley
⅔ cup beef stock
1 egg, beaten

Serves 4

1

Roll out two-thirds of the pastry on a floured surface to about ⅛-inch thick. Line a 6-cup pie dish. Place a pie funnel in the middle.

2

Put the flour, salt and pepper in a bowl and toss the cubes of steak in the mixture. Remove all fat and skin from the kidneys, and slice thickly. Add to the steak cubes and toss well. Melt the butter in a pan and fry the chopped onion until soft, then add the mustard, bay leaves, parsley and stock and stir well.

3

Preheat the oven to 375°F. Place the steak and kidney in the pie and add the stock mixture. Roll out the remaining pastry to a thickness of ⅛ inch. Brush the edges of the pastry forming the lower half of the pie with beaten egg and cover with the second piece of pastry. Press the pieces of pastry together to seal the edges, then trim. Use the trimmings to decorate the top with a pattern of leaves.

4

Brush the whole pie with beaten egg and make a small hole over the top of the funnel. Bake for about 1 hour, until the pastry is golden brown.

Veal Kidneys with Mustard

This dish is equally delicious made with lamb kidneys. Be sure not to cook the sauce too long after adding the mustard or it will lose its piquancy.

INGREDIENTS

*2 veal kidneys or 8–10 lamb kidneys,
skinned
2 tablespoons butter
1 tablespoon vegetable oil
1 cup button mushrooms, quartered
¼ cup chicken stock
2 tablespoons brandy (optional)
¾ cup crème fraîche or heavy cream
2 tablespoons Dijon mustard
salt and freshly ground black pepper
snipped fresh chives, to garnish*

Serves 4

3

Add the mushrooms to the pan and sauté for 2–3 minutes, until golden, stirring frequently. Pour in the chicken stock and brandy, if using, then bring to a boil and boil for 2 minutes.

4

Stir in the cream and cook for about 2–3 minutes, until the sauce is slightly thickened. Stir in the mustard and seasoning, then add the kidneys and cook for 1 minute. Sprinkle with the chives before serving.

1

Cut the kidneys into pieces, discarding any fat. If using lamb kidneys, remove the central core by cutting a V shape from the middle of each kidney, then cut each kidney into three or four pieces.

2

Melt the butter with the oil in a large frying pan. Add the kidneys, sauté over high heat for 3–4 minutes, stirring frequently, until well browned, then transfer them to a plate using a slotted spoon.

White Veal Stew

In France, this "white" farmhouse stew is known as a blanquette because it is enriched with cream and egg yolks. It is traditionally made with veal, but can be made with lamb.

INGREDIENTS

*3–3½ pounds boneless veal shoulder,
cut into 2-inch cubes
6 cups veal or chicken stock
1 large onion, studded with 2 cloves
4 carrots, sliced
2 leeks, sliced
1 garlic clove, halved
1 bouquet garni
1 tablespoon black peppercorns
5 tablespoons butter
2 cups button mushrooms, quartered if
large
1½ cups shallots or pearl onions*

*1 tablespoon sugar
⅓ cup all-purpose flour
½ cup crème fraîche or heavy cream
pinch of grated nutmeg
¼ cup chopped fresh dill or parsley
salt and white pepper
fresh herb sprigs, to garnish*

Serves 6

1

Put the veal and stock in a large, flameproof casserole. Bring to a boil, skim the surface, then add the studded onion, one of the sliced carrots, the leeks, garlic, bouquet garni and peppercorns. Cover, lower the heat and simmer for about 1 hour, until the veal is just tender.

2

Meanwhile, melt 1 tablespoon of the butter in a frying pan and sauté the mushrooms until lightly golden. Transfer to a large bowl, using a slotted spoon.

3

Melt another 1 tablespoon of the butter in the pan and add the shallots or onions. Sprinkle with the sugar and add about 6 tablespoons of the veal cooking liquid. Cover and simmer for 10–12 minutes, until the onions are tender and the liquid has evaporated. Add the onions to the mushrooms.

4

When the veal is tender, transfer the cubes to the bowl of vegetables using a slotted spoon. Strain the veal cooking liquid and discard the cooked vegetables and bouquet garni, then wash the casserole and return it to the heat.

5

Melt the remaining butter, add the flour and cook for 1–2 minutes. Gradually whisk in the reserved cooking liquid. Bring to a boil, then lower the heat and simmer the sauce until smooth and slightly thickened. Add the remaining carrots and cook for another 10 minutes, until tender.

6

Whisk the cream into the sauce and simmer until slightly thickened. Add the meat, mushrooms and onions and simmer for 10–15 minutes, until the veal is very tender. Season with salt, white pepper and a little nutmeg, then stir in the chopped dill or parsley. Garnish with fresh herb sprigs and serve.

Desserts

When it comes to desserts, farmhouse cooks are fortunate. They may need to go no further than the orchard to pick scented apples, pears or bright red cherries. Stalks of rhubarb, sweet soft fruits and juicy plums are theirs for the taking. No wonder their desserts are so delicious. The following pages offer an abundance of ideas to serve as a final course for anything from a family meal to a formal dinner party.

Lemon Meringue Bombe with Mint Chocolate

This easy ice cream will cause a sensation at a dinner party—it is unusual, but the most delicious combination of tastes that you can imagine.

INGREDIENTS

2 large lemons
1 cup sugar
3 small sprigs fresh mint
⅔ cup whipping cream
2½ cups plain yogurt
2 large meringues
8 ounces good-quality mint chocolate,
grated

Serves 6–8

1

Slice the rind off the lemons with a potato peeler, then squeeze them for juice. Place the lemon rind and sugar in a food processor and blend finely. Add the cream, yogurt and lemon juice and process thoroughly. Pour the mixture into a mixing bowl and add the meringues, roughly crushed.

3

When the ice cream has frozen, scoop out the middle and pour in the grated mint chocolate. Replace the ice cream to cover the chocolate and refreeze.

2

Reserve one of the mint sprigs and chop the rest finely. Add to the mixture. Pour into a 5-cup glass bowl and freeze for 4 hours.

4

To turn out, dip the bowl in very hot water for a few seconds to loosen the ice cream, then turn the bowl upside down over the serving plate. Decorate with grated chocolate and a sprig of mint.

Apple Mint and Pink Grapefruit Fool

Apple mint can easily run riot in the herb garden; this is an excellent way of using up an abundant crop.

INGREDIENTS

1 pound tart apples, peeled, cored and sliced
8 ounces pink grapefruit segments
3 tablespoons honey
2 tablespoons water
6 large sprigs apple mint, plus more to garnish
²⁄₃ cup heavy cream
1¹⁄₃ cup custard

Serves 4–6

1

Place the apples, grapefruit, honey, water and apple mint in a pan, cover and simmer for 10 minutes, until soft. Leave in the pan to cool, then discard the apple mint. Purée the mixture in a food processor.

2

Whip the cream until it forms peaks and fold into the custard, keeping 2 tablespoons to decorate. Carefully fold the cream into the fruit mixture. Serve chilled and decorated with swirls of cream and sprigs of mint.

Country Strawberry Fool

Make this delicious fool on the day you want to eat it, and chill it well,
for the best strawberry taste.

INGREDIENTS

1 1/4 cups milk
2 egg yolks
scant 1/2 cup superfine
sugar
few drops of vanilla extract
2 lb ripe strawberries, stemmed
and washed
juice of 1/2 lemon
1 1/4 cups heavy cream

To decorate
12 small strawberries
4 fresh mint sprigs

Serves 4

1

First make the custard. Whisk 2 tbsp milk
with the egg yolks, 1 tbsp superfine sugar
and the vanilla extract.

2

Heat the remaining milk until it is just
below boiling point.

3

Stir the milk into the egg mixture. Rinse
the pan out and return the mixture to it.

4

Gently heat and stir until the custard
thickens enough to coat the back of a wooden
spoon. Lay a wet piece of wax paper on the
top of the custard and let it cool.

5

Purée the strawberries in a food processor or
blender with the lemon juice and the
remaining sugar.

6

Lightly whip the cream and fold in the fruit
purée and custard. Pour into glass dishes and
decorate with the whole strawberries and
sprigs of mint.

Orange-blossom Mold

A fresh orange gelatin mold makes a delightful dessert: the natural fruit flavor combined with the smooth gelatin has a clean taste that is especially welcome after a rich main course. This is delicious served with thin, crisp cookies.

INGREDIENTS

5 tbsp superfine sugar
²/₃ cup water
2 packets of gelatin
(about 1 oz)
2½ cups freshly squeezed
orange juice
2 tbsp orange-flower water

Serves 4–6

1

Place the superfine sugar and water in a small saucepan and gently heat to dissolve the sugar. Leave to cool.

2

Sprinkle the gelatin over ensuring it is completely dissolved in the water. Let stand until the gelatin has absorbed all the liquid and is solid.

3

Gently melt the gelatin over a bowl of simmering water until it becomes clear and transparent. Leave to cool. When the gelatin is cold, mix it with the orange juice and orange-flower water.

4

Wet a mold and pour in the gelatin. Chill in the refrigerator for at least 2 hours, or until set. Turn out to serve.

Steamed Ginger and Cinnamon Syrup Pudding

A traditional and comforting steamed pudding, best served with custard.

INGREDIENTS

9 tbsp softened butter
3 tbsp maple syrup
½ cup superfine sugar
2 eggs, lightly beaten
1 cup all-purpose flour
1 tsp baking powder
1 tsp ground cinnamon
1 oz preserved ginger,
finely chopped
2 tbsp milk
custard, to serve

Serves 4

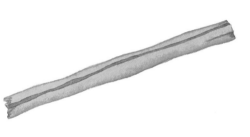

1

Set a full steamer or saucepan of water on to boil. Lightly grease a 2½ cup pudding bowl with 1 tbsp butter. Place the maple syrup in the bowl.

2

Cream the remaining butter and sugar together until light and fluffy. Gradually add the eggs until the mixture is glossy. Sift the flour, baking powder and cinnamon together and fold them into the mixture, with the preserved ginger. Add the milk to make a soft, dropping consistency.

3

Spoon the batter into the bowl and smooth the top. Cover with a pleated piece of wax paper, to allow for expansion during cooking. Tie securely with string and steam for 1½–2 hours, making sure that the water level is kept topped up, to ensure a good flow of steam to cook the pudding. Turn the pudding out to serve it.

Poached Pears

Use a firm, sweet pear such as Bartlett or Anjou and serve warm.

INGREDIENTS

6 medium pears
1¾ cups superfine
sugar
3 tbsp honey
1 vanilla bean
2½ cups red wine
1 tsp whole cloves
3 in cinnamon stick
whipped cream to serve

Serves 4

1

Peel the pears but leave them whole,
keeping the stalks as well.

2

Put the sugar, honey, vanilla bean, wine,
cloves and cinnamon stick in a large pan.

3

Add the pears and poach until soft, about
30 minutes. When the pears are tender,
remove them with a slotted spoon and keep
them warm. Remove the vanilla bean, cloves
and cinnamon stick and boil the liquid
until it is reduced by half. Serve spooned
over the pears.

Cherry Clafoutis

This wonderful way of serving fresh cherries is part of French farmhouse traditions.

INGREDIENTS

6 cups fresh cherries
½ cup all-purpose flour
pinch of salt
4 eggs, plus 2 egg yolks
½ cup sugar, plus extra for dusting
2½ cups milk
4 tablespoons melted butter, plus extra for greasing

Serves 6

1

Preheat the oven to 375°F. Lightly butter the bottom and sides of a shallow ovenproof dish. Pit the cherries and place them in a single layer in the dish.

2

Sift the flour and salt into a bowl. Add the eggs, egg yolks, sugar and a little of the milk and whisk to a smooth batter.

3

Gradually whisk in the rest of the milk and the melted butter, then pour the batter over the cherries. Bake for 40–50 minutes, until golden and just set. Serve warm, dusted with sugar.

NOTE
If fresh cherries are not available, use two 15-ounce cans pitted black cherries, thoroughly drained. For a special dessert, add 3 tablespoons kirsch or cherry brandy to the batter.

Mint Ice Cream

*This ice cream is best served slightly softened, so take it out
of the freezer 20 minutes before you want to serve it. For a special occasion,
this looks spectacular served in an ice bowl.*

INGREDIENTS

*8 egg yolks
6 tbsp superfine sugar
2½ cups light cream
1 vanilla bean
4 tbsp chopped fresh mint,
to garnish*

Serves 8

—— 1 ——

Beat the egg yolks and sugar until they are
pale and light using a hand-held electric
beater or a balloon whisk. Transfer to a
small saucepan.

—— 2 ——

In a separate saucepan, bring the cream to
a boil with the vanilla bean.

—— 3 ——

Remove the vanilla bean and pour the
hot cream on to the egg mixture,
whisking briskly.

—— 4 ——

Continue whisking to ensure the eggs
are mixed into the cream.

—— 5 ——

Gently heat the mixture until the custard
thickens enough to coat the back of a
wooden spoon. Let cool.

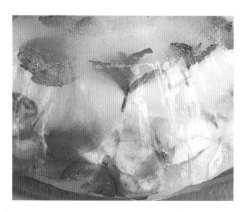

—— 6 ——

Stir in the mint and place in an ice-cream
maker to churn, about 3–4 hours. If you
don't have an ice-cream maker, freeze the
ice cream until mushy and then whisk it well
again, to break down the ice crystals. Freeze
for another 3 hours until it is softly frozen
and whisk again. Finally freeze until hard:
at least 6 hours.

Summer Fruit Gâteau with Heartsease

No one can resist the appeal of little heartsease pansies. This cake would be lovely for a sentimental summer occasion in the garden.

INGREDIENTS

8 tablespoons margarine, plus more to
grease mold
3¾ ounces sugar
2 teaspoons honey
1¼ cup self-rising flour
½ teaspoon baking powder
2 tablespoons milk
2 eggs, plus white of one more for
crystallizing
1 tablespoon rose water
1 tablespoon Cointreau
16 heartsease flowers
superfine sugar, as required, to
crystallize
confectioners' sugar, to decorate
1 pound strawberries
strawberry leaves, to decorate

1

Crystallize the heartsease pansies by painting them with lightly beaten egg white and sprinkling with superfine sugar. Let dry.

2

Preheat the oven to 375°F. Grease and lightly flour a ring mold.

3

In a large mixing bowl, mix the soft margarine, sugar, honey, flour, baking powder, milk and 2 eggs and beat well for 1 minute. Add the rose water and the Cointreau and mix well.

4

Pour the mixture into the pan and bake for 40 minutes. Let stand for a few minutes and then turn out onto the plate that you wish to serve it on.

5

Sift confectioners' sugar over the cake. Fill the center of the ring with strawberries. Decorate with crystallized heartsease flowers and some strawberry leaves.

Borage, Mint and Lemon Balm Sorbet

Borage has such a pretty flower head that it is worth growing just to make this recipe, and to float the flowers in summer drinks. The sorbet itself has a very refreshing, delicate taste, perfect for a hot afternoon.

INGREDIENTS

1 pound sugar
2 cups water
6 sprigs mint, plus more to decorate
6 lemon balm leaves
1 cup white wine
2 tablespoons lemon juice
borage sprigs, to decorate

Serves 6–8

1

Place the sugar and water in a saucepan with the washed herbs. Bring to a boil. Remove from the heat and add the wine. Cover and cool. Chill for several hours, then add the lemon juice. Freeze, and as soon as the mixture begins to freeze, stir briskly and replace in the freezer. Repeat every 15 minutes for at least 3 hours.

3

Place a small freezer-proof bowl inside each larger bowl and put inside a heavy weight, such as a metal weight from some scales. Fill with more cooled boiled water, float more herbs in this, and freeze.

2

To make the small ice bowls, pour about ½ inch cold, boiled water into small freezer-proof bowls about 2½ cups in capacity, and arrange some herbs in the water. Freeze, then add a little more water to cover the herbs.

4

To release the ice bowls, warm the inner bowl with a small amount of very hot water and twist it out. Warm the outer bowl by standing it in very hot water for a few seconds, then turn out the ice bowl. Spoon the sorbet into the ice bowls and decorate with sprigs of mint and borage.

Blackberry Charlotte

A classic dessert, perfect for cold days. Serve with lightly whipped cream or homemade custard.

INGREDIENTS

5 tbsp unsalted butter
3 cups fresh white bread crumbs
4 tbsp brown sugar
4 tbsp maple syrup
finely grated rind and juice
of 2 lemons
2 oz walnut halves
1 lb blackberries
1 lb cooking apples, peeled,
cored and finely sliced
whipped cream or
custard, to serve

Serves 4

1

Preheat the oven to 350°F. Grease a 2 cup
Pyrex dish with 1 tbsp of the butter. Melt the
remaining butter and add the bread crumbs.
Sauté them for 5–7 minutes, until the
crumbs are slightly crisp and golden.
Leave to cool slightly.

2

Place the sugar, syrup, lemon rind and juice
in a small saucepan and gently warm them.
Add the crumbs.

3

Process the walnuts until they are
finely ground.

4

Arrange a thin layer of blackberries in the
dish. Top with a thin layer of crumbs.

5

Add a thin layer of apple, topping it with
another thin layer of crumbs. Repeat the
process with another layer of blackberries,
followed by a layer of crumbs. Continue
until you have used up all the ingredients,
finishing with a layer of crumbs.
The mixture should be piled well above
the top edge of the dish, because it shrinks
during cooking. Bake for 30 minutes, until
the crumbs are golden and the fruit is soft.

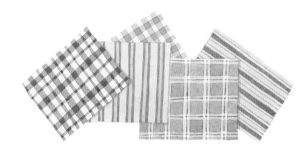

Mixed Berry Tart

The orange-flavored pastry is delicious with the fresh fruits of summer.
Serve this with some extra shreds of orange rind scattered on top.

INGREDIENTS

For the pastry
2 cups all-purpose flour
½ cup unsalted butter
finely grated rind of 1 orange,
plus extra to decorate

For the filling
1¼ cups crème fraîche
and ¾ cup whipped cream
or ¾ cup sour cream
finely grated rind of 1 lemon
2 tsp confectioner's sugar
1½ lb mixed summer
berries

Serves 8

1

To make the pastry, put the flour and butter
in a large bowl. Rub in the butter until the
mixture resembles bread crumbs.

2

Add the orange rind and enough cold water
to make a soft dough.

3

Roll into a ball and chill for at least
30 minutes. Roll out the pastry on a
lightly floured surface.

4

Line a 9 in loose-based quiche pan with
the pastry. Chill for 30 minutes. Preheat the
oven to 400°F and place a baking sheet in
the oven to heat up. Line the pan with
wax paper and baking beans and bake blind
on the baking sheet for 15 minutes. Remove
the paper and beans and bake for 10 minutes
more, until the pastry is golden. Allow to
cool completely. To make the filling,
whisk the crème fraîche, lemon rind and
sugar together and pour into the pastry crust.
Top with fruit, sprinkle with orange
rind and serve sliced.

French Apple Tart

For added flavor, scatter some slivered almonds over the top of this classic tart.

INGREDIENTS

For the pastry
½ cup unsalted butter,
softened
4 tbsp vanilla sugar
1 egg
2 cups all-purpose flour

For the filling
4 tbsp unsalted butter
5 large tart apples, peeled, cored
and sliced
juice of ½ lemon
1¼ cups heavy cream
2 egg yolks
2 tbsp vanilla sugar
⅔ cup ground almonds,
toasted
2 tbsp slivered almonds, toasted,
to garnish

Serves 8

1
─────

Place the butter and sugar in a food processor
and process them well together. Add the egg
and process to mix it in well.

2
─────

Add the flour and process till you have a
soft dough. Wrap the dough in plastic wrap
and chill it for 30 minutes.

3
─────

Roll the pastry out on a lightly floured
surface to about 9–10 in diameter.

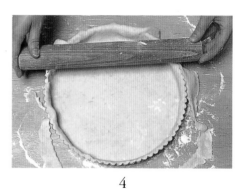

4
─────

Line a pie pan with the pastry and chill it
for a further 30 minutes. Preheat the oven
to 425°F and place a baking sheet in the
oven to heat up. Line the pastry case with
wax paper and baking beans and bake blind
on the baking sheet for 10 minutes. Then
remove the beans and paper and cook for
a further 5 minutes.

5
─────

Turn the oven down to 375°F. To make the
filling, melt the butter in a frying pan and
lightly sauté the apples for 5–7 minutes.
Sprinkle the apples with lemon juice.

6
─────

Beat the cream and egg yolks with the sugar.
Stir in the toasted ground almonds. Arrange
the apple slices on top of the warm pastry
and pour over the cream mixture. Bake for
25 minutes, or until the cream is just about
set – it tastes better if the cream is still
slightly runny in the center. Serve hot or cold,
scattered with slivered almonds.

Spiced Red Fruit Compote

When summer fruits are at their best, what could be nicer than a simple compote?

INGREDIENTS

4 ripe red plums, halved
2 cups strawberries, halved
1¼ cups raspberries
2 tablespoons light brown sugar
2 tablespoons cold water
1 cinnamon stick
3 pieces of star anise
6 cloves
plain yogurt or fromage frais, to serve

Serves 4

1

Place all the ingredients, except the yogurt or fromage frais, in a heavy pan. Heat gently, without boiling, until the sugar dissolves and the fruit juices run.

2

Cover the pan and let the fruit infuse over very low heat for about 5 minutes. Remove the spices from the compote before serving warm with plain yogurt or fromage frais.

Rhubarb Cobbler

Typical English farmhouse fare: stewed rhubarb with biscuit topping.

INGREDIENTS

1½ pounds rhubarb, sliced
3 tablespoons orange juice
6 tablespoons granulated sugar
1¾ cups self-rising flour
1 cup plain yogurt
grated rind of 1 medium orange
2 tablespoons light-brown sugar
1 teaspoon ground ginger
plain yogurt or custard, to serve

Serves 4

1

Preheat the oven to 400°F. Cook the rhubarb, orange juice and ¼ cup of the granulated sugar over low heat. Transfer to an ovenproof dish.

2

To make the topping, mix the flour with the remaining granulated sugar, then gradually stir in enough of the yogurt to bind to a soft dough.

3

Roll out the dough on a floured surface to a 10-inch square. Combine the orange rind, brown sugar and ginger, then sprinkle over the dough.

4

Roll up the dough quite tightly, then cut into about ten slices. Arrange the dough slices over the rhubarb.

5

Bake the cobbler for 15–20 minutes, or until golden brown. Serve warm with plain yogurt.

Rhubarb and Orange Crumble

The almonds give this crumble topping a nutty taste and crunchy texture.
This crumble is extra-delicious with home-made custard.

INGREDIENTS

2 lb rhubarb, cut in
2 in lengths
6 tbsp superfine sugar
finely grated rind and juice
of 2 oranges

1 cup all-purpose flour
½ cup unsalted butter,
chilled and cubed
6 tbsp demerara sugar
1¼ cups ground almonds

Serves 6

1

Preheat the oven to 350°F. Place the rhubarb
in a shallow ovenproof dish.

2

Sprinkle the superfine sugar over and add the
orange rind and juice.

3

Sift the flour into a mixing bowl and add the
butter. Rub the butter into the flour until
the mixture resembles bread crumbs.

4

Add the demerara sugar and ground almonds
and mix well.

5

Spoon the crumble mixture over the fruit to
cover it completely. Bake for 40 minutes,
until the top is browned and the fruit is
cooked. Serve warm.

Christmas Pudding

The classic Christmas dessert. Wrap it in cheesecloth and store it in an airtight container for up to a year for the flavors to develop.

INGREDIENTS

1 cup all-purpose flour
pinch of salt
1 tsp ground allspice
½ tsp ground cinnamon
¼ tsp freshly grated nutmeg
1 cup grated hard Crisco
1 apple, grated
2 cups fresh white
bread crumbs
1⅞ cups soft brown
sugar
2 oz slivered almonds
1½ cups seedless raisins
1½ cups currants
1½ cups golden raisins
4 oz ready-to-eat dried
apricots
¾ cup chopped mixed
citrus peel
finely grated rind and juice
of 1 lemon
2 tbsp molasses
3 eggs
1¼ cups milk
2 tbsp rum

Serves 8

<u>1</u>

Sift the flour, salt and spices into
a large bowl.

<u>2</u>

Add the Crisco, apple and other dry
ingredients, including the grated
lemon rind.

<u>3</u>

Heat the molasses until warm and runny
and pour into the dry ingredients.

<u>4</u>

Mix together the eggs, milk, rum
and lemon juice.

<u>5</u>

Stir the liquid into the dry mixture.

<u>6</u>

Spoon the mixture into two 5 cup bowls.
Wrap the puddings with pieces of wax paper,
pleated to allow for expansion, and tie with
string. Steam the puddings in a steamer or
saucepan of boiling water. Each pudding
needs 10 hours' cooking and 3 hours'
reheating. Remember to keep the water level
topped up to keep the pans from boiling dry.
Serve decorated with holly.

Baking

When the aroma of newly baked bread and cakes is in the air, everyone makes a beeline for the kitchen. The anticipation of feasting on these delights is almost as enjoyable as the eating. The following section provides a selection of traditional breads, cakes, tarts and other baked goods that will be enjoyed by all the family time and time again.

The Harvest Loaf

The centerpiece for celebrations when the harvest is safely gathered in, the harvest loaf is a potent symbol of country life. It is too salty to eat, but looks wonderful. Although there were many different designs of harvest loaf, the most enduringly popular was the wheatsheaf, symbolic as it is of the harvest and the vital importance of bread as "the staff of life."

INGREDIENTS

14 cups white bread flour
2 tablespoons salt
2 x ¼-ounce envelopes active dry yeast
3–3¾ cups lukewarm water
beaten eggs, to glaze

Makes two 1¾-pound loaves

1

Sift the flour and salt into a large mixing bowl and stir in the yeast. Add enough warm water to make a rough dough. Knead on a lightly floured surface for about 10 minutes, until smooth and elastic. Place the dough in a lightly oiled bowl, cover and let rise for 1–2 hours, until it has doubled in bulk.

2

Preheat the oven to 425°F. Oil and flour a large baking sheet. Roll out about 8 ounces of the dough into a 12-inch-long cylinder. Place it on the baking sheet and flatten slightly with your hand. This will form the body of the bread, symbolizing the long stalks of the wheatsheaf. The high salt content in the dough makes it easier to work, but the bread is more decorative than palatable.

3

Roll and shape about 12 ounces of the remaining dough into a crescent; place this at the top of the cylinder and flatten. Divide the remaining dough in half. Take one half and divide it in two again. Use one half to make the stalks of the wheat by rolling into narrow ropes and placing on the "stalk" of the sheaf. Use the other half to make a braid to decorate the finished loaf where the stalks meet the ears of

4

Use the remaining dough to make the ears of wheat. Roll it into small sausage shapes and snip each a few times with scissors to give the effect of the separate ears. Place these on the crescent shape, fanning out from the base until the wheatsheaf is complete. Position the braid between the stalks and the ears of wheat. Brush the wheatsheaf with the beaten egg. Bake for 20 minutes, then reduce the heat to 325°F and bake for 20 minutes more.

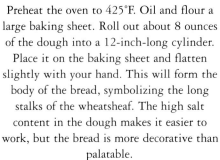

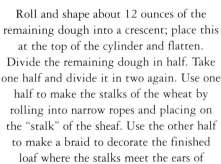

Olive Bread

Olive breads are popular all over the Mediterranean. For this Greek recipe, use rich, oily olives or those marinated in herbs, rather than canned ones.

INGREDIENTS

2 red onions
2 tablespoons olive oil
1⅓ cups pitted black or green olives
7 cups white bread flour
1½ teaspoons salt
4 teaspoons active dry yeast
3 tablespoons coarsely chopped fresh parsley, cilantro or mint
2 cups lukewarm water

Makes two 1½-pound loaves

VARIATION
Shape the dough into 16 small rolls. Slash the tops as below and reduce the cooking time to 25 minutes.

1
Slice the onions thinly. Sauté them gently in the oil until soft. Coarsely chop the olives.

2
Put the flour, salt, yeast and parsley, cilantro or mint in a large bowl. Stir in the olives and fried onions, then pour in the warm water. Mix to a dough, adding a little more water if the mixture feels dry.

3
Knead on a lightly floured surface for about 10 minutes, until smooth and elastic. Cut the dough in half. Shape into two rounds and place on two oiled baking sheets. Cover loosely with lightly oiled plastic wrap and leave until doubled in size.

4
Preheat the oven to 425°F. Slash the tops of the loaves with a knife. Bake for about 40 minutes, or until the loaves sound hollow when tapped on the bottom. Transfer to a wire rack to cool.

Potato Bread

Mashed potatoes make a lovely loaf. Make sure that the liquid is only warm, not hot, when added.

8 ounces potatoes, peeled and halved or
quartered
2 tablespoons vegetable oil
1 cup lukewarm milk
6 cups white bread flour
1 tablespoon salt
4 teaspoons active dry yeast

Makes 2 loaves

1

Cook the potatoes in a saucepan of salted water for 20–30 minutes. Drain and reserve the cooking water. Return the potatoes to the pan and mash with oil and milk. Mix the flour, salt and yeast together. Put the potato mixture in a bowl. Stir in 1 cup of the potato cooking water, then gradually stir in the flour mixture to form a stiff dough.

2

Knead the dough for 10 minutes. Grease two 9 x 5-inch loaf pans. Roll the dough into 20 small balls. Place two rows of balls in each pan. Cover with plastic wrap and leave in a warm place to rise. Preheat the oven to 400°F. Bake the loaves for 10 minutes, then lower the heat to 375°F and bake for about 40 minutes more.

Irish Soda Bread

This traditional farmhouse loaf needs no rising, so it's perfect for unexpected guests.

INGREDIENTS

2 cups all-purpose white flour, plus
extra for dusting
1 cup whole-wheat flour
1 teaspoon baking soda
1 teaspoon salt
2 tablespoons butter, softened
1¼ cups buttermilk

Makes 1 loaf

1

Preheat the oven to 400°F. Grease a baking sheet. Sift the dry ingredients into a bowl. Make a well in the center and add the butter and buttermilk. Gradually incorporate the surrounding flour to make a soft dough. Gather the dough into a ball. Knead the dough on a floured surface for 3 minutes. Shape into a round.

2

Place the round on the baking sheet. Cut a cross in the top with a sharp knife. Dust with flour, then bake for 40–50 minutes, or until golden brown. Transfer to a rack to cool.

Easter Braid

Serve this delicious bread sliced with butter and jam.
It is also very good toasted on the day after you made it.

INGREDIENTS

7/8 cup milk
2 eggs, lightly beaten
6 tbsp superfine sugar
4 cups all-purpose flour
1/2 tsp salt
2 tsp ground allspice
6 tbsp butter
3/4 oz fresh yeast

1 1/4 cups currants
1/4 cup candied mixed citrus
peel, chopped
a little sweetened milk, to glaze
1 1/2 tbsp candied cherries,
chopped
1 tbsp angelica, chopped

Serves 8

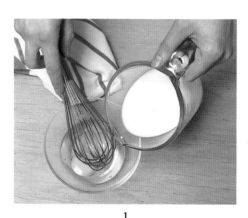

1

Warm the milk to lukewarm, add two-thirds
of it to the eggs and mix in the sugar.

2

Sift the flour, salt and allspice together.
Rub in the butter. Make a well in the center
of the flour, add the milk and yeast, adding
more milk as necessary to make a sticky dough.

3

Knead on a well-floured surface and then
knead in the currants and mixed peel,
reserving 1 tbsp for the topping. Put the
dough in a lightly greased bowl and cover
it with a damp dish towel. Let rise until
double its size. Preheat the oven to 425°F.

4

Turn the dough out on to a floured surface
and knead again for 2–3 minutes. Divide the
dough into three even pieces. Roll each
piece into a sausage shape roughly
8 in long. Braid the three pieces together,
turning under and pinching each end. Place
on a floured baking sheet and let rise
for 15 minutes.

5

Brush the top with sweetened milk and
scatter with coarsely chopped cherries, strips
of angelica and the reserved peel. Bake in the
preheated oven for 45 minutes or until the
bread sounds hollow when tapped on the
bottom. Cool slightly on a wire rack.

Whole Wheat Bread

Homemade bread creates one of the most evocative smells in country cooking.
Eat this on the day you bake it, to enjoy the superb fresh taste.

INGREDIENTS

¾ oz fresh yeast
1¼ cups lukewarm milk
1 tsp superfine sugar
1½ cups whole wheat flour,
sifted
2 cups all-purpose white flour,
sifted
1 tsp salt
4 tbsp butter, chilled and cubed
1 egg, lightly beaten
2 tbsp mixed seeds

Makes 4 round loaves or
2 long loaves

1

Gently dissolve the yeast with a little of the milk and the sugar to make a paste. Place both the flours plus any bran from the sifter and the salt in a large warmed mixing bowl. Rub in the butter until the mixture resembles bread crumbs.

2

Add the yeast mixture, remaining milk and egg and mix into a fairly soft dough. Knead on a floured board for 15 minutes. Lightly grease the mixing bowl and put the dough back in the bowl, covering it with a piece of greased plastic wrap. Let rise until double in size in a warm place (this should take at least an hour).

3

Punch the dough down and knead it for a further 10 minutes. Preheat the oven to 400°F. To make round loaves, divide the dough into four pieces and shape them into flattish rounds. Place them on a floured baking sheet and let rise for a further 15 minutes. Sprinkle the loaves with the mixed seeds. Bake for about 20 minutes until golden and firm.

NOTE

For pan-shaped loaves, put the punched-down dough into two greased loaf pans instead. Let rise for a further 45 minutes and then bake for about 45 minutes, until the loaf sounds hollow when turned out of the pan and knocked on the base.

Scones

The secret of making scones is not to overwork the dough.

1

Preheat the oven to 425°F. Sift the dry ingredients into a mixing bowl. Mix in the butter or margarine with a fork until the mixture resembles coarse bread crumbs.

2

Add the buttermilk and mix swiftly to a soft dough.

3

Knead the dough on a lightly floured board for 30 seconds.

4

Roll or pat out the dough to a thickness of ½ inch. Use a floured 2½-inch pastry cutter to cut out 10 rounds. Transfer the rounds to a baking sheet and bake for 10–12 minutes, until well risen and golden brown.

Cheese Scones

These delicious scones make a good tea-time or brunch treat. They are best served fresh and still slightly warm.

INGREDIENTS

2 cups all-purpose flour
2½ tsp baking powder
½ tsp mustard powder
½ tsp salt
4 tbsp butter, chilled and cubed
3 oz Cheddar cheese, grated
⅔ cup milk
1 egg, beaten

Makes 12

1

Preheat the oven to 450°F. Sift the flour, baking powder, mustard powder and salt into a mixing bowl. Add the butter and rub it into the flour mixture until the mixture resembles bread crumbs. Stir in 2 oz of the cheese.

2

Make a well in the center and add the milk and egg. Mix gently and then turn the dough out on to a lightly floured surface. Roll it out and cut it into triangles or squares. Brush lightly with milk and sprinkle with the remaining cheese. Let rest for 15 minutes, then bake them for 15 minutes, or until well risen.

Oatcakes

These are very simple to make and are an excellent addition to a cheese board.

INGREDIENTS

1⅔ cups oatmeal
¾ cup all-purpose flour
¼ tsp baking soda
tsp salt
2 tbsp Crisco
2 tbsp butter

Makes 24

1

Preheat the oven to 425°F. Place the oatmeal, flour, soda and salt in a large bowl. Gently melt the Crisco and butter together in a pan.

2

Add the melted fat and enough boiling water to make a soft dough. Turn out on to a surface scattered with a little oatmeal. Roll out the dough thinly and cut it into circles. Bake the oatcakes on ungreased baking sheets for 15 minutes, until crisp.

Cranberry Muffins

A tea or breakfast dish that is not too sweet.

INGREDIENTS

3 cups all-purpose flour
1 tsp baking powder
pinch of salt
1/2 cup superfine sugar
2 eggs
2/3 cup milk
4 tbsp corn oil
finely grated rind of 1 orange
5 oz cranberries

Makes 12

1

Preheat the oven to 375°F. Line a muffin pan with paper cases. Mix the flour, baking powder, salt and superfine sugar together.

2

Lightly beat the eggs with the milk and oil. Add them to the dry ingredients and blend to make a smooth batter. Stir in the orange rind and cranberries. Divide the mixture between the muffin cases and bake for 25 minutes until risen and golden. Let cool in the pan for a few minutes, and serve warm or cold.

Country Pancakes

Serve these hot with butter and maple syrup or jam.

INGREDIENTS

2 cups self-rising flour
4 tbsp superfine sugar
4 tbsp butter, melted
1 egg
1 1/4 cups milk
1 tbsp corn oil or
margarine

Makes 24

1

Mix the flour and sugar together. Add the melted butter and egg with two-thirds of the milk. Mix to a smooth batter – it should be thin enough to find its own level.

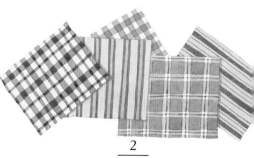

2

Heat a griddle or a heavy-based frying pan and wipe it with a little oil or margarine. When hot, drop spoonfuls of the mixture on to the hot griddle or pan. When bubbles come to the surface of the pancakes, flip them over to cook until golden on the other side. Keep the pancakes warm wrapped in a dish towel while cooking the rest of the mixture. Serve as soon as possible.

Butter Cookies

These little cookies are similar to shortbread, but richer.
Handle them with care, because they break easily.

INGREDIENTS

12 tablespoons (1½ sticks) butter,
diced, plus extra for greasing
6 egg yolks, lightly beaten
1 tablespoon milk
2 cups all-purpose flour
¾ cup sugar

Makes 18–20

1

Preheat the oven to 350°F. Lightly butter a large, heavy baking sheet. Mix 1 tablespoon of the beaten egg yolks with the milk to make a glaze, then set aside.

2

Sift the flour into a large bowl and make a well in the center. Add the remaining egg yolks, sugar and butter and, using your fingertips, work them together until smooth and creamy.

3

Gradually incorporate the flour to make a smooth, slightly sticky dough.

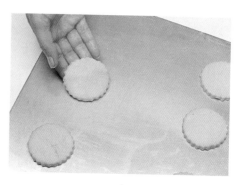

4

Using floured hands, pat out the dough to a thickness of ⅜ inch and cut out rounds using a 3-inch cutter. Transfer the rounds to a baking sheet, brush each with a little egg glaze, then, using the back of a knife, score to create a lattice pattern.

5

Bake for 12–15 minutes, until golden. Cool on the baking sheet on a wire rack for 15 minutes, then carefully remove the cookies and let cool completely on the rack.

Orange Shortbread Fingers

These are a real tea-time treat. The fingers will keep in an airtight tin for up to two weeks.

INGREDIENTS

½ cup unsalted butter,
softened
4 tbsp superfine sugar,
plus a little extra
finely grated rind of 2 oranges
1 ½ cups all-purpose flour

Makes 18

1

Preheat the oven to 375°F. Beat the butter and sugar together until they are soft and creamy. Beat in the orange rind.

2

Gradually add the flour and gently pull the dough together to form a soft ball. Roll the dough out on a lightly floured surface until about ½ in thick. Cut it into fingers, sprinkle over a little extra superfine sugar, prick with a fork and bake for about 20 minutes, or until the fingers are a light golden color.

Pound Cake

This orange-scented cake is good for dessert with a fruit sauce.

INGREDIENTS

3 cups fresh raspberries, strawberries
or pitted cherries, or a combination of
any of these
1 cup sugar, plus extra for sprinkling
1 tablespoon lemon juice
1½ cups all-purpose flour
2 teaspoons baking powder
pinch of salt
12 tablespoons (1½ sticks) butter,
softened
3 eggs
grated zest of 1 orange
1 tablespoon orange juice

Serves 6–8

1

Reserve a few whole fruits for decorating.
In a food processor fitted with the metal
blade, process the remaining fruit until
smooth. Add 2 tablespoons of the sugar and
the lemon juice, then process again to
combine. Strain the sauce and chill.

2

Line the bottom of and grease an 8 x 4-inch
loaf pan. Sprinkle the bottom and sides of
the pan lightly with sugar and pour out
any excess. Preheat the oven to 350°F .

3

Sift the flour with the baking powder and
salt. In a medium bowl, beat the butter
until creamy. Add the remaining sugar and
beat for 4–5 minutes, until very light and
fluffy. Add the eggs, one at a time, beating
well after each addition. Beat in the orange
zest and juice.

4

Gently fold in the flour mixture in batches,
then spoon the mixture into the prepared
pan and tap gently to release any air
bubbles. Bake for 35–40 minutes, until the
top of the cake is golden and springs back
when touched. Cool in the pan for
10 minutes, then transfer the cake to a wire
rack and cool for 30 minutes more. Remove
the lining paper and serve slices or wedges
of the warm cake with a little of the fruit
sauce. Decorate with the reserved fruit.

Dark Fruitcake

With its colorful citrus and candied fruit topping, this tasty cake needs no further decoration.

INGREDIENTS

1 cup currants
1 cup raisins
²/₃ cup golden raisins
¹/₄ cup candied cherries, halved
3 tablespoons Madeira or sherry
12 tablespoons (1¹/₂ sticks) butter
1 cup dark brown sugar
2 extra large eggs
1³/₄ cups all-purpose flour
2 teaspoons baking powder
2 teaspoons each ground ginger,
allspice and cinnamon
1 tablespoon molasses
1 tablespoon milk
¹/₄ cup candied fruit, chopped
1 cup walnuts or pecans, chopped

For the decoration
1 cup granulated sugar
¹/₂ cup water
1 lemon, thinly sliced
¹/₂ orange, thinly sliced
¹/₂ cup orange marmalade
candied cherries

Serves 12

4

Spoon into the pan, spreading out so there is
a slight well in the center of the mixture.
Bake for 2½–3 hours, until a skewer inserted
in the cake comes out clean. Cover with foil
when the top is golden to prevent
overbrowning. Cool in the pan on a rack.

5

To decorate, mix the sugar and water in a
saucepan and bring to a boil. Add the
citrus slices and cook for 20 minutes.
Remove the fruit with a slotted spoon.
Pour the remaining syrup over the cake and
leave to cool. Melt the marmalade, then
brush over the top of the cake. Decorate
with the candied citrus fruit and cherries.

1

Mix the currants, raisins, golden raisins and
cherries in a bowl. Stir in the Madeira or
sherry. Cover and leave overnight.

2

Preheat the oven to 300°F. Line and grease
a 9-inch round springform pan. Cream
the butter and sugar in a mixing bowl
until light and fluffy. Beat in the eggs,
one at a time.

3

Sift together the flour, baking powder and
spices. Fold into the butter mixture in
batches. Fold in the molasses, milk, dried
fruit and liquid, candied fruit and nuts.

Light Fruitcake

This is not the conventional fruitcake mixture, but it is moist, rich and absolutely delicious.

INGREDIENTS

1¹⁄₃ cups prunes
1¹⁄₃ cups dates
1¹⁄₃ cups currants
1¹⁄₃ cups golden raisins
1 cup dry white wine
1 cup rum
3 cups all-purpose flour
2 teaspoons baking powder
1 teaspoon ground cinnamon
¹⁄₂ teaspoon grated nutmeg
16 tablespoons (2 sticks) butter,
at room temperature
1 cup sugar
4 eggs, lightly beaten
1 teaspoon vanilla extract

Makes 2 loaves

1

Pit the prunes and dates and chop finely. Place in a bowl with the currants and golden raisins. Stir in the wine and rum. Cover and let stand for 48 hours. Stir occasionally.

2

Preheat the oven to 300°F. Line and grease two 9 x 5-inch loaf pans. Sift the flour, baking powder, cinnamon and nutmeg into a bowl.

3

Cream the butter and sugar together until light and fluffy. Gradually add the eggs and vanilla extract. Fold in the flour mixture in batches, then add the dried fruit mixture and its liquid. Mix lightly.

4

Divide the mixture between the pans and bake for about 1½ hours, or until a skewer inserted in a loaf comes out clean. Cool in the pan for 20 minutes, then transfer to a wire rack to cool completely.

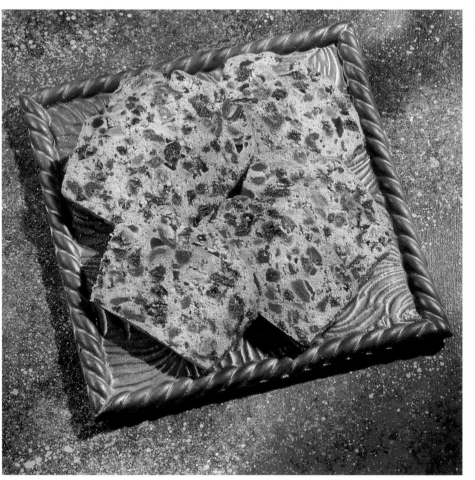

BAKING

Lemon Drizzle Cake

You can also make this recipe using a large orange instead of the lemons; either way, it makes a zesty treat for afternoon tea.

INGREDIENTS

finely grated rind of 2 lemons
³/₄ cup superfine sugar
1 cup unsalted butter,
softened
4 eggs
2 cups self-rising flour
1 tsp baking powder
¹/₄ tsp salt
shredded rind of 1 lemon,
and 1 tsp granulated sugar
to decorate

For the syrup
juice of 1 lemon
³/₄ cup superfine sugar

Serves 6

1

Preheat the oven to 325°F. Grease a 2 lb loaf pan or 7–8 in round cake pan and line it with wax paper or baking parchment. Mix the lemon rind and superfine sugar together.

2

Cream the butter with the lemon and sugar mixture. Add the eggs and mix until smooth. Sift the flour, baking powder and salt into a bowl and fold a third at a time into the mixture. Turn the batter into the pan, smooth the top and bake for 1¹/₂ hours or until golden brown and springy to the touch.

3

To make the syrup, slowly heat the juice with the sugar and dissolve it gently. Make several slashes in the top of the cake and pour the syrup over. Sprinkle the shredded lemon rind and 1 tsp granulated sugar on top and leave to cool.

Farmhouse Carrot Cake

Marvelously moist and full of flavors, carrot cake has become a true classic.

INGREDIENTS

2 cups granulated sugar
1 cup vegetable oil
4 eggs
4 medium carrots, finely grated
2 cups all-purpose flour
1½ teaspoons baking soda
1½ teaspoons baking powder
1 teaspoon ground allspice
1 teaspoon ground cinnamon

For the icing
2 cups confectioners' sugar
1 cup cream cheese, softened
4 tablespoons (½ stick) butter, softened
2 teaspoons vanilla extract
1½ cups walnuts or pecans, chopped

Serves 10

1

In a bowl, combine the granulated sugar, oil, eggs and carrots. Beat for 2 minutes.

2

Sift the dry ingredients into another bowl. Add in batches to the carrot mixture, mixing well after each addition. Preheat the oven to 375°F. Grease and flour two 9-inch round layer-cake pans.

3

Divide the batter evenly between the prepared cake pans. Bake for 35–45 minutes, or until a skewer inserted in the center of a cake comes out clean. Cool in the pans for 10 minutes, then transfer the cakes to wire racks to cool completely.

4

For the icing, beat all the ingredients in a bowl until smooth. Sandwich the layers together with one-third of the icing, then spread the remaining icing over the top and sides of the cake, swirling it to make a decorative finish. Sprinkle the nuts around the rim.

Maple Walnut Pie

This pie is deliciously naughty—but nice.

INGREDIENTS

3 eggs
salt
¹⁄₄ cup sugar
4 tablespoons (¹⁄₂ stick) butter, melted
1 cup pure maple syrup
1 cup walnuts, chopped
whipped cream, to decorate

For the pastry
¹⁄₂ cup all-purpose flour
¹⁄₂ cup whole-wheat flour
4 tablespoons (¹⁄₂ stick) butter, diced
3 tablespoons vegetable shortening, diced
1 egg yolk
2–3 tablespoons ice water

Serves 8

1

For the pastry, mix the flours and a pinch of salt in a bowl. Rub in the butter and shortening until the mixture resembles bread crumbs. Stir in the egg yolk and just enough water to bind the dough. Gather it into a ball, wrap in waxed paper and chill for 20 minutes.

2

Preheat the oven to 425°F. On a lightly floured surface, roll out the dough and line a 9-inch pie pan. Trim the edge. To decorate, roll out the trimmings and stamp out small heart shapes. Brush the edge of the pastry shell with water, then arrange the dough hearts around the rim.

3

Prick the bottom of the pastry shell with a fork. Line with crumpled foil and bake for 10 minutes. Remove the foil and bake for 3–6 minutes more, until golden brown.

4

In a bowl, whisk the eggs, a pinch of salt and the sugar together. Stir in the melted butter and maple syrup. Put the pastry shell on a baking sheet. Pour in the filling, then sprinkle the nuts over the top. Bake for 35 minutes, or until just set. Cool on a rack. Decorate with whipped cream.

Lemon Meringue Pie

This tasty pie would make a perfect end to a simple summer picnic. Served cold, it needs no accompaniment.

INGREDIENTS

grated zest and juice of 1 large lemon
1 cup water
2 tablespoons (¼ stick) butter
1 cup sugar
3 tablespoons cornstarch mixed to a
paste with 1 tablespoon water
3 eggs, separated
pinch each of salt and cream of tartar

For the pastry
1 cup all-purpose flour
½ teaspoon salt
6 tablespoons vegetable shortening,
diced
2 tablespoons ice water

Serves 8

NOTE
For Lime Meringue Pie, substitute the grated zest and juice of 2 medium-size limes for the lemon.

1

For the pastry, sift the flour and salt into a bowl. Rub in the shortening until the mixture resembles bread crumbs. Stir in water to bind the dough and roll out.

2

Line a 9-inch pie pan with the pastry, allowing the pastry to overhang the edge by ½ inch. Fold the overhang under and crimp the edges. Chill the pastry shell for at least 20 minutes. Preheat the oven to 400°F.

3

Prick the pastry all over with a fork. Line with crumpled foil and bake for 12 minutes. Remove the foil and bake for 6–8 minutes more, until golden.

4

In a saucepan, combine the lemon rind and juice with the water. Add the butter and ½ cup of the sugar. Bring the mixture to a boil. Mix the cornstarch paste with the egg yolks. Add to the lemon mixture and return to a boil, whisking constantly for about 5 minutes, until the mixture thickens. Cover the surface with damp waxed paper to prevent a skin from forming. Let cool.

5

For the meringue, beat the egg whites with the salt and cream of tartar until they hold stiff peaks. Add the remaining sugar and beat until glossy.

6

Spoon the lemon mixture into the pastry shell and level it. Spoon the meringue on top, smoothing it up to the edge of the pastry to seal. Bake for 12–15 minutes, or until the meringue is tinged with gold.

The Farmhouse Pantry

Walk into the farmhouse pantry and discover a wonderful array of pickles, chutneys, jams and jellies. There are flavored oils, too, and cheeses packed in olive oil to be given as gifts or saved for special occasions. The colors are glorious, the contents superb. The following section provides recipes that will allow you to enjoy the fruits of your labor all year round.

Tomato Chutney

This spicy chutney is delicious with a selection of cheeses and biscuits,
or with cold meats.

INGREDIENTS

2 lb tomatoes, skinned	1 ⅛ cups superfine sugar
1 ⅓ cups raisins	2 ½ cups cider
8 oz onions, chopped	vinegar

Makes 4 × 1 lb jars

1

Chop the tomatoes coarsely. Put them in
a preserving pan.

2

Add the raisins, onions and sugar.

3

Pour over the vinegar. Bring to a boil
and let it simmer for 2 hours, uncovered.
Pot into sterilized jars. Seal with a waxed disc
and cover with a tightly fitting plastic
top. Store in a cool, dark place. The chutney
will keep unopened for up to a year. Once
opened, store in the fridge and consume
within a week.

Green Apple Chutney

This family recipe is wonderful with broiled sausages and baked ham.

INGREDIENTS

2¼ pounds green apples
3–4 garlic cloves
4 cups malt vinegar
2⅔ cups dates, chopped
⅔ cup preserved ginger, chopped
2⅔ cups raisins
2⅔ cups brown sugar
½ teaspoon cayenne pepper
2 tablespoons salt

Makes about 6 pounds

1

Cut the unpeeled apples into quarters, remove the cores and chop coarsely. Peel and chop the garlic and place it in a saucepan with the apples.

2

Pour in the vinegar and boil until the apples are soft. Add all the other ingredients. Boil gently for 45 minutes. Spoon the mixture into warm, sterilized jars. Seal with melted paraffin and cover with a tightly fitting cellophane top.

Green Tomato Chutney

Unripened tomatoes are a culinary success rather than a horticultural failure when transformed into a delicious chutney.

INGREDIENTS

2 onions, chopped
2¼ pounds green tomatoes, quartered
1 pound apples, cored and chopped, but not peeled
4 cups malt vinegar
2½ cups brown sugar
1½ cups golden raisins
1½ teaspoons mustard powder
1 teaspoon ground cinnamon
¼ teaspoon ground cloves
¼ teaspoon cayenne pepper

Makes about 5½ pounds

1

Place the chopped onions in a large preserving pan. Add the tomatoes and apples. Stir in all the remaining ingredients and heat gently, stirring until the sugar has dissolved.

2

Bring to a boil, then simmer uncovered, stirring occasionally, for 1½ hours. Pour into warm, sterilized jars. Seal with melted paraffin and cover with a cellophane top.

Windfall Pear Chutney

The apparently unusable bullet-hard pears that litter the ground underneath old pear trees after high winds are ideal for this tasty chutney.

INGREDIENTS

1½ pounds pears, peeled and cored
3 onions, chopped
1 cup raisins
1 cooking apple, cored and chopped
⅓ cup preserved ginger
1 cup walnuts, chopped
1 garlic clove, chopped
grated zest and juice of 1 lemon
2½ cups cider vinegar
1 cup brown sugar
2 cloves
1 teaspoon salt

Makes about 4½ pounds

1

Chop the pears roughly and put them in a bowl. Add the onions, raisins, apple, ginger, walnuts and garlic, with the lemon zest and juice. Put the vinegar, sugar, cloves and salt in a saucepan. Gently heat, stirring until the sugar has dissolved, then bring to a boil briefly and pour in the fruit. Cover and let sit overnight.

2

Pour the mixture into a preserving pan and boil gently for 1½ hours, until soft. Spoon into warm, sterilized jars. Seal with melted paraffin and cover with a cellophane top.

Tarragon and Champagne Mustard

This delicate mustard is very good with cold seafood.

INGREDIENTS

2 tablespoons mustard seeds
5 tablespoons champagne vinegar
1 cup mustard powder
²/₃ cup brown sugar
¹/₂ teaspoon salt
3¹/₂ tablespoons virgin olive oil
¹/₄ cup fresh tarragon, chopped

Makes about 9 ounces

1

Soak the mustard seeds overnight in the vinegar. Pour the mixture into a blender, add the mustard powder, sugar and salt and blend until smooth. With the motor running, gradually add the oil through the hole in the lid until completely blended. With the motor off, stir in the tarragon. Pour the mustard into sterilized jars, seal and store in a cool place.

Honey Mustard

Richly flavored honey mustard is delicious in sauces and salad dressings.

INGREDIENTS

1¹/₂ cups mustard seeds
1 tablespoon ground cinnamon
¹/₂ teaspoon ground ginger
1¹/₄ cups white wine vinegar
6 tablespoons dark honey

Makes about 1¹/₄ pounds

1

Mix the mustard seeds and spices in a bowl, pour in the vinegar and let soak overnight. Place the mixture in a mortar and pound to a paste. Gradually work in the honey. The finished mustard should resemble a stiff paste, so add extra vinegar if necessary. Store the mustard in sterilized jars in the refrigerator. Use within 4 weeks.

Horseradish Mustard

Horseradish mustard is a tangy relish that is an excellent accompaniment to cold meats, smoked fish or cheese.

INGREDIENTS

3 tablespoons mustard seeds
1 cup boiling water
1 cup mustard powder
¹/₂ cup sugar
¹/₂ cup white wine or cider vinegar
¹/₄ cup olive oil
1 teaspoon lemon juice
2 tablespoons horseradish sauce

Makes about 14 ounces

1

Place the mustard seeds in a heatproof bowl, pour the boiling water over them and let sit for 1 hour. Drain, then put in a blender. Add the remaining ingredients and blend the mixture to a smooth paste. Spoon it into sterilized jars. Store in the refrigerator and use within 3 months.

Mint Sauce

Mint sauce is the classic accompaniment to roast lamb.

INGREDIENTS

1 large bunch mint
½ cup boiling water
⅔ cup wine vinegar
2 tablespoons sugar

Makes 1 cup

1

Chop the mint finely and place it in a 2½-cup pitcher. Pour in the boiling water and let sit to infuse. When lukewarm, add the vinegar and sugar. Pour into a clean bottle and store in the refrigerator.

Ketchup

The true tomato taste shines through in this homemade sauce.

INGREDIENTS

5–5¼ pounds very ripe tomatoes
1 onion
6 cloves
4 allspice berries
6 black peppercorns
1 fresh rosemary sprig
1 ounce fresh ginger, sliced
1 celery heart, chopped
2 tablespoons brown sugar
4 tablespoons raspberry vinegar
3 garlic cloves, peeled
1 tablespoon salt

Makes 6 pounds

1

Skin and seed the tomatoes, then chop them finely and place in a large saucepan. Stud the onion with the cloves, tie it with the allspice, peppercorns, rosemary and ginger in a double layer of cheesecloth and add to the saucepan. Stir in the celery, sugar, vinegar, garlic and salt.

2

Bring the mixture to a boil over high heat, stirring occasionally. Reduce the heat and simmer for 1½–2 hours, stirring frequently, until reduced by half. Purée the mixture in a blender or food processor, then return to the pan and bring to a boil. Reduce the heat and simmer for 15 minutes, then pour into clean, sterilized jars. Store in the refrigerator. Use within 2 weeks.

Traditional Horseradish Sauce

Fresh horseradish root is extremely potent, but its effects can be alleviated if it is scrubbed and peeled underwater and a food processor is used to do the fine chopping or grating.

INGREDIENTS

3 tablespoons horseradish root, freshly grated
1 tablespoon white wine vinegar
1 teaspoon superfine sugar
pinch of salt
⅔ cup thick heavy cream, for serving

Makes about ¾ cup

1

Place the grated horseradish in a bowl. Stir in the vinegar, sugar and a pinch of salt.

2

Pour the sauce into a sterilized jar. It can be kept for up to 6 months in the refrigerator. A couple of hours before you intend to serve it, stir in the cream.

OPPOSITE: *Each of these sauces is a powerful reduction of its main ingredients.*

Mushrooms Preserved in Oil

The method of preserving in oil is ideally suited to good-quality, firm mushrooms. The oil takes on a delicious mushroom flavor, and can be used to make special salad dressings.

INGREDIENTS

1 cup white wine vinegar
⅔ cup water
1 teaspoon salt
1 fresh thyme sprig
½ bay leaf
1 fresh red chili (optional)
1 pound assorted wild mushrooms
1⅔ cups virgin olive oil

Makes 2 cups

1

Bring the vinegar and water to a simmer in a stainless-steel pan. Add the salt, thyme, bay leaf and chili (if using). Infuse for 15 minutes. Add the mushrooms.

2

Simmer for 10 minutes. Drain the mushrooms thoroughly, then spoon them into a sterilized preserving jar.

3

Cover the mushrooms with oil, close the lid and label. Mushrooms in oil will keep in a cool place for up to 12 months.

Spiced Mushrooms in Vodka

Mushrooms combine with caraway seeds, lemon and chili to make this unusual aperitif.

INGREDIENTS

3 ounces chanterelle and oyster mushrooms
1 teaspoon caraway seeds
1 lemon
1 fresh red chili
1½ cups vodka

Makes 1½ cups

1

Place the mushrooms, caraway seeds, lemon and whole chili in a clean preserving jar or bottle.

2

Pour in the vodka and leave for 2–3 weeks, until the mushrooms no longer float. Chill thoroughly before straining and serving.

Pickled Mushrooms

Pickled mushrooms not only look good on the pantry shelf, they also taste delicious, especially when dressed with a little olive oil. In this recipe, shiitake mushrooms take on an Asian flavor, but other firm mushrooms and spices can be used.

INGREDIENTS

1 cup white wine vinegar
⅔ cup water
1 teaspoon salt
1 fresh red chili
2 teaspoons coriander seeds
2 teaspoons szechuan pepper
9 ounces shiitake mushrooms, halved if large

Makes 2 cups

1

Bring the wine vinegar and water to a simmer in a stainless-steel pan. Add the salt, whole chili, coriander seeds, szechuan pepper and mushrooms and cook for 10 minutes.

2

Spoon the mushrooms and liquid into a sterilized 2¼-cup preserving jar. Seal, label and let sit for at least 10 days before trying.

Chanterelle Vodka

For an unusual aperitif, try steeping chanterelle mushrooms in vodka. Chill well before straining and serving.

INGREDIENTS

1½ cups vodka
3 ounces young chanterelle mushrooms, trimmed

Makes 1½ cups

1

Place the chanterelle mushrooms in a clean preserving bottle or jar.

2

Pour in the vodka, cover and leave at room temperature. Chanterelle vodka is ready when the mushrooms have dropped to the bottom.

Piccalilli

The piquancy of this relish partners well with sausages, bacon or ham.

INGREDIENTS

1½ lb cauliflower   1 tsp dry mustard powder
1 lb small onions   2 tsp corn starch
12 oz green beans   2½ cups vinegar
1 tsp ground turmeric

Makes 3 × 1 lb jars

1

Cut the cauliflower into tiny florets.

2

Peel the onions and top and tail
the green beans.

3

In a small saucepan, measure in the turmeric,
mustard powder and corn starch, and pour
over the vinegar. Stir well and simmer
for 10 minutes.

4

Pour the vinegar mixture over the vegetables
in a pan, mix well and simmer
for 45 minutes.

5

Pour into sterilized jars. Seal each jar with a
waxed disc and a tightly fitting plastic
top. Store in a cool dark place. The piccalilli
will keep unopened for up to a year. Once
opened store in the fridge and consume
within a week.

Dill Pickles

*Dill is easy to grow and is a delightful herb. It goes well with fish and gives
a superb flavor to this popular pickle.*

INGREDIENTS

6 small cucumbers
2 cups water
4 cups white wine vinegar
½ cup salt
3 bay leaves
3 tablespoons dill seed
2 garlic cloves, slivered

Makes about 10 cups

1

Slice the cucumbers into medium-thick slices. Put the water, vinegar and salt in a saucepan. Bring to a boil, then immediately remove from the heat.

2

Layer the herbs and garlic between slices of cucumber in sterilized preserving jars until the jars are full, then cover with the warm salt and vinegar mixture. When the liquid is cold, close the jars. Leave on a sunny windowsill for at least 1 week before using.

Rhubarb and Ginger-Mint Jam

Ginger and mint are easily grown in the garden, and they are just the thing to boost the flavor of rhubarb jam.

INGREDIENTS

4½ pounds rhubarb
1 cup water
juice of 1 lemon
2-inch piece of fresh ginger, peeled and bruised, plus 2–3 tablespoons fresh ginger, very finely chopped
6 cups sugar
⅔ cup preserved ginger, chopped mint leaves

Makes about 6 pounds

NOTE
To confirm the setting point, spoon a little of the jam onto a cold saucer. Let sit for 2 minutes. A skin should have formed on the jam that will wrinkle if you push it gently with your finger.

1

Cut the rhubarb into short lengths. Place the rhubarb, water and lemon juice in a preserving pan and bring to a boil. Peel and bruise the fresh ginger and add to the pan. Reduce the heat and simmer, stirring frequently, until the rhubarb is soft.

2

Remove the ginger. Add the sugar and stir until dissolved. Boil for 10–15 minutes, or until setting point is reached. Skim off scum from the surface of the jam, then add the preserved ginger, the chopped fresh ginger and the mint leaves. Pour into sterilized glass jars, seal with melted paraffin and cover with tightly fitting cellophane tops.

Apple and Mint Jelly

This jelly is delicious served with garden peas, as well as the more traditional rich roasted meat such as lamb.

INGREDIENTS

2 lb cooking apples
granulated sugar
3 tbsp chopped fresh mint

Makes 3 × 1 lb jars

1

Chop the apples coarsely and put them in a preserving pan.

2

Add enough water to cover. Simmer until the fruit is soft.

3

Pour through a jelly bag, allowing it to drip overnight. Do not squeeze the bag or the jelly will become cloudy.

4

Measure the amount of juice. To every 2½ cups of juice, add 2¾ cups granulated sugar.

5

Place the juice and sugar in a large pan and heat gently. Dissolve the sugar and then bring to a boil. Test for setting, by pouring about 1 tbsp into a saucer and leaving to cool slightly. If a wrinkle forms on the surface when pushed with a fingertip, the jelly will set. When a set is reached, leave to cool.

6

Stir in the mint and pour into sterilized jars. Seal each jar with a waxed disc and a tightly fitting plastic top. Store in a cool, dark place. The jelly will keep unopened for up to a year. Once opened, keep in the fridge and consume within a week.

Rosemary-flavored Oil

This pungent oil is ideal drizzled over meat or vegetables before grilling.

INGREDIENTS

2½ cups olive oil
5 fresh rosemary sprigs

Makes 2½ cups

1

Heat the oil until warm but not too hot.

2

Add four rosemary sprigs and heat gently.
Put the reserved rosemary sprig in a clean
bottle. Strain the oil, pour in the bottle and
seal tightly. Allow to cool and store in a
cool, dark place. Use within a week.

Thyme-flavored Vinegar

This vinegar is delicious sprinkled over salmon intended for poaching.

INGREDIENTS

*2½ cups white-wine
vinegar*
5 fresh thyme sprigs
3 garlic cloves, peeled

Makes 2½ cups

1

Warm the vinegar.

2

Add four thyme sprigs and the garlic and
heat gently. Put the reserved thyme sprig in
a clean bottle, strain the vinegar, and add to
the bottle. Seal tightly, allow to cool and
store in a cool, dark place. The vinegar
may be kept unopened for up to 3 months.

Yogurt Cheese in Olive Oil

Simple cheese making has always been a farmhouse tradition.
This recipe comes from Greece and is based on yogurt made from sheep's milk.

INGREDIENTS

3½ cups Greek sheep-milk yogurt
2½ teaspoons salt
2 teaspoons dried chilies, crushed, or
chili powder
1 tablespoon fresh rosemary, chopped
1 tablespoon fresh thyme or oregano,
chopped
about 1¼ cups olive oil, preferably
garlic-flavored

Makes about 2 pounds

NOTE
If your kitchen is particularly warm, find a cooler place to suspend the cheese. Alternatively, drain the cheese in the refrigerator, suspending the bag from one of the shelves.

1

Sterilize a 12-inch square of cheesecloth by steeping it in boiling water. Drain and lay over a large plate. Mix the yogurt with the salt and place in the center of the cheesecloth. Bring up the sides of the cheesecloth and tie firmly with string.

2

Suspend the bag from a kitchen cupboard handle or similar suitable hook, allowing a bowl to be placed underneath to catch the whey. Leave for 2–3 days, until the yogurt stops dripping.

3

Combine the chilies and herbs. Take teaspoonfuls of the cheese and roll into balls with your hands. Carefully lower into two sterilized 1-pound glass preserving jars, sprinkling each layer with some of the herb mixture.

4

Pour the oil over the cheese until completely covered. Store in the refrigerator for up to 3 weeks. To serve the cheese, spoon out of the jars with a little of the flavored olive oil and spread on slices of lightly toasted bread.

Preserved Cherry Tomatoes

Cherry tomatoes bottled in their own juices are the perfect accompaniment to country ham.

INGREDIENTS

2¼ pounds cherry tomatoes
salt (see method)
sugar (see method)
fresh basil leaves

5 garlic cloves per jar

Makes 2¼ pounds

1

Preheat the oven to 250°F. Prick each tomato with a toothpick.

2

Pack the tomatoes into clean, dry 4-cup preserving jars, adding 1 teaspoon each of salt and sugar to each jar.

3

Fill the jars to within ¾ inch of the top, tucking the basil leaves and garlic among the tomatoes. Rest the lids on the jars, but do not seal. Set on a baking sheet lined with a layer of cardboard or newspaper and place in the oven. After about 45 minutes, when the juice is simmering, remove from the oven and seal. Store in the refrigerator and use within 6 months.

Pickled Beets

The rich color and intense flavor of pickled beets make them a perennial favorite.

INGREDIENTS

1 pound beets, cooked and peeled
1 large onion, sliced
1¼ cups cider vinegar
⅔ cup water
¼ cup sugar

Makes 1 pound

1

Slice the beets and pack them into a sterilized jar, layering with the sliced onion. Pour the vinegar and water into a saucepan. Add the sugar and bring to a boil.

2

Pour the liquid over the beets and seal the jar. Store in a cool place and use within 1 month, or longer if kept in the refrigerator.

Lemon and Lime Curd

Serve this creamy, tangy spread with toast or muffins,
instead of jam, for a delightful change.

INGREDIENTS

¹/₂ cup unsalted butter	grated rind and juice of 2 lemons
	grated rind and juice of 2 limes
3 eggs	1 ¹/₈ cups superfine sugar

Makes 2 × 1 lb jars

1

Set a heatproof mixing bowl over a large pan
of simmering water. Add the butter.

2

Lightly beat the eggs and add them
to the butter.

3

Add the lemon and lime rinds and juices,
then add the sugar.

4

Stir the mixture constantly until it thickens.
Pour into sterilized jars. Seal each jar with a
waxed disc and a tightly fitting plastic top.
Store in a cool, dark place. The curd will
keep unopened for up to a month.
Once opened, keep in the fridge and
consume within a week.

Strawberry Jam

This classic recipe is always popular. Make sure the jam is allowed to cool before pouring into jars so the fruit doesn't float to the top.

INGREDIENTS

3–3 ½ lb strawberries
juice of ½ lemon
3–3 ½ lb granulated sugar

Makes about 5 lb

1

Hull the strawberries.

2

Put the strawberries in a pan with the lemon juice. Mash a few of the strawberries. Let the fruit simmer for 20 minutes or until softened.

3

Add the sugar and let it dissolve slowly over a gentle heat. Then let the jam boil rapidly until a setting point is reached.

4

Let stand until the strawberries are well distributed through the jam. Pack into sterilized jars. Seal each jar with a waxed disc and cover with a tightly fitting plastic top. Store in a cool dark place. The jam may be kept unopened for up to a year. Once opened, keep in the fridge and consume within a week.

Crab Apple Jelly

Crab apple trees are so pretty with their abundant flowers and glowing red fruit, and though their role in the garden is mainly decorative, this jelly is a delicious way to make use of the fruit.

INGREDIENTS

*2¼ pounds crab apples
3 cloves
water (see method)
granulated sugar (see method)*

**Makes about 2¼ pounds from each
2½ cups liquid**

1

Wash the apples and cut them in half but do not peel or core. Place the apples and cloves in a large saucepan and pour in water to cover. Bring to a boil, reduce the heat and simmer until the apples are soft.

2

Strain the mixture through cheesecloth or a jelly bag into a bowl. Put the sugar in a heatproof bowl in the oven for 15 minutes. Measure the juice and add 2 cups sugar for each 2 cups of juice. Pour into a pan and heat gently. Stir until the sugar dissolves, then boil rapidly until the setting point is reached. Pour into warm, sterilized jars and seal.

Rose Hip and Apple Jelly

This recipe uses windfall apples and rose hips gathered from the rose garden. The jelly is rich in vitamin C as well as full of flavor.

INGREDIENTS

*2¼ pounds windfall apples, peeled, trimmed and quartered
1 pound firm, ripe rose hips
1¼ cups boiling water
granulated sugar (see method)*

**Makes about 2¼ pounds from each
2½ cups liquid**

1

Place the quartered apples in a preserving pan with just enough water to cover them. Bring to a boil and cook until the apples are pulpy. Meanwhile, chop the rose hips coarsely in a food processor. Add the rose hips to the cooked apples with the boiling water. Leave to simmer for 10 minutes, then remove from the heat and allow to stand for 10 minutes more. Pour the mixture into a thick jelly bag suspended over a bowl and leave to strain overnight.

2

Preheat the oven to 250°F. Measure the juice and allow 1¾ cups sugar for each 2½ cups of liquid. Warm the sugar in the oven. Pour the juice into a pan and bring to a boil, stir in the warmed sugar until it has dissolved completely, then let boil until a setting point is reached. Finally, pour the jelly into warm, sterilized jars and seal securely.

Three-fruit Marmalade

Homemade marmalade may be time-consuming but the results are incomparably better than storebought varieties.

INGREDIENTS

12 oz oranges
12 oz lemons
1½ lb grapefruit
10¼ cups water
6 lb granulated sugar

Makes 6 × 1 lb jars

1

Rinse the fruit and dry them.

2

Put the fruit in a preserving pan. Add the water and let it simmer for about 2 hours.

3

Quarter the fruit, remove the pulp and add it to the pan with the cooking liquid.

4

Cut the rinds into slivers, and add to the pan. Add the sugar. Gently heat until the sugar has dissolved. Bring to a boil and cook until a setting point is reached. Let stand for 1 hour to allow the peel to settle. Pour into sterilized jars. Seal each jar with a waxed disc and a tightly fitting plastic top. Store in a cool, dark place.

Poached Spiced Plums in Brandy

*Canning spiced fruit is a great way to preserve summer flavors for eating
in winter. Serve these with whipped cream as a dessert.*

INGREDIENTS

*2½ cups brandy
rind of 1 lemon, peeled in a
long strip
1⅔ cups superfine sugar
1 cinnamon stick
2 lb fresh plums*

Makes 2 lb

1

Put the brandy, lemon rind, sugar and
cinnamon stick in a large pan and heat gently
to dissolve the sugar. Add the plums and
poach for 15 minutes, or until soft.
Remove with a slotted spoon.

2

Reduce the syrup by a third by rapid boiling.
Strain it over the plums. Pack the plums
in large sterilized jars. Seal tightly and store
for up to 6 months in a cool, dark place.

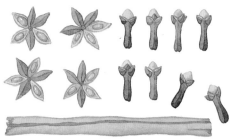

Spiced Pickled Pears

*These delicious pears are the perfect accompaniment for cooked ham
or cold meat salads.*

INGREDIENTS

*2 lb pears
2½ cups white-wine
vinegar
1⅛ cups superfine sugar
1 cinnamon stick
5 star anise
10 whole cloves*

Makes 2 lb

1

Peel the pears, keeping them whole
and leaving on the stalks. Heat the vinegar
and sugar together until the sugar has melted.
Pour over the pears and poach for 15 minutes.

2

Add the cinnamon, star anise and cloves
and simmer for 10 minutes. Remove the
pears and pack tightly into sterilized jars.
Simmer the syrup for a further 15 minutes
and pour it over the pears. Seal the jars
tightly and store in a cool, dark place. The
pears will keep for up to a year unopened.
Once opened, store in the fridge and
consume within a week.

Peach Wine

This delicious wine is intended to be made and drunk during the summer,
either on its own or diluted with soda water.

INGREDIENTS

6 ripe peaches
4 cups dry white wine
1 cup superfine sugar
³/₄ cup fruit brandy

Makes about 5 cups

1

Peel the peaches, cut them in half and
remove the pits. Put them in a pan with
the white wine and poach for about
15 minutes, until tender. Cover and allow
to stand overnight.

2

Remove the peaches, then strain the liquid
through a coffee filter. Add the sugar and
fruit brandy and stir to dissolve the sugar.
Pour the liquid into clean, dry, sterilized
bottles and cork. Store in the refrigerator.
Drink within 2 weeks. Serve well chilled.

Mulberry Liqueur

If you can't find mulberries, blackberries also make a delicious drink.

INGREDIENTS

mulberries
superfine sugar
vodka, brandy or gin

1

Fill clean, dry, sterilized jars with clean
fruit. Pour in superfine sugar so that it
comes one-third of the way up the jar, then
fill to the top with the spirit of your choice.
Seal the jars and shake them to help the
sugar dissolve. Store for at least 2 months.

2

Strain off the fruit (which you can use to
make a delicious apple pie) and bottle the
liqueur in clean, dry, sterilized bottles and
seal securely. It should keep indefinitely if
stored in airtight bottles.

Sloe Gin

This is a real country drink. Sloes are gathered after the first frosts, and the first bottle is
ready for Christmas. Black plums can be used if sloes are not available.

INGREDIENTS

sloes
superfine sugar
gin

1

Wash the sloes and remove the stems.
Prick each sloe with a toothpick or needle, then
pack the fruit into a wide-necked jar or bottle.
Pour in superfine sugar so that it comes halfway
up the jar, then fill to the top with gin and seal.

2

Shake the jar from time to time to help the
sugar dissolve. Before drinking, strain off
the sloes and decant the liquid into a pretty
bottle that is clean and dry.

Index